my JOY JOURNEY
JOURNEY
with Amy

my JOY JOURNEY with Amy

A LOVE STORY THROUGH LIFE, LOSS, GRIEF, AND *healing*

MARK D. YOUNGQUIST

My Joy Journey With Amy: A Love Story Through Life, Loss, Grief, and Healing

Copyright © 2025 Mark D. Youngquist

First edition, 2025

Published by Mark D. Youngquist

ISBN: 979-8-9926399-1-9 (Hard Cover)

ISBN: 979-8-9926399-0-2 (Paperback)

ISBN: 979-8-9926399-2-6 (eBook)

Library of Congress Control Number: 2025910245

Editing by Melissa Stevens, Purple Ninja Editorial
www.PurpleNinjaEditorial.com

Cover design and interior layout by Becky's Graphic Design®, LLC
www.BeckysGraphicDesign.com

Stock photos licensed from istockphoto.com (istock by Getty Images)

All other photos are the personal property of Mark D. Youngquist

For the love of my life, Amy.

You brought so much joy to my life.
I miss you every hour, every minute, and
every second of each and every day.

CONTENTS

PREFACE

THERE IS NO MANUAL for how to handle a cancer diagnosis or for the journey through treatments. Neither for the grief many families experience when the outcome results in the loss of a loved one. Loss is a profound, life-changing event that has no end. I will not pretend to have any tidy answers for you on how to overcome grief or to provide a process for you to follow in your own grief journey. I simply do not have one, even for myself.

This book is about my joy journey with the love of my life, Amy. You probably are curious about the use of the word *joy* in describing this journey. Certainly, cancer is not a joyful event, but the word *joy* had special meaning and significance to Amy and, because of her example, to many others. After receiving her cancer diagnosis, Amy expressed very adamantly that she wanted to somehow find joy in our cancer journey as well. As you read this collection of reflections, I think you will come to understand the joy Amy sought. Throughout this book, I will be recalling the many wonderful, joyful memories of my life with Amy as well as chronicling my own challenges and struggles through grief to healing.

I do not want to rehash our cancer journey for you from beginning to end in painful detail. I'm not sure I could. The short version is that Amy was diagnosed with cancer of unknown primary (CUP). This meant they could not identify through biopsy, scans, molecular classifier, or genetic sequencing the origin of her cancer. She was diagnosed in July 2021. She underwent radiation and chemotherapy and responded well to treatment for nearly a year. In September 2022, her disease began to progress rapidly, and she passed away from complications on October 24, 2022. If you feel that you want to know additional details, I will simply refer you to her CaringBridge site (www.caringbridge. org/site/3486d88e-5de0-3b6a-bc85-98d48e1272a8), which I have opened up to all viewers. It documents our cancer journey in more detail.

I have also decided not to tell our story in chronological order for a simple reason: I undertook this writing initiative in large part as a therapeutic exercise. Many of these chapters are reflections either from my hiking or from shared memories with family and friends. Some reflections come from other family members who have chosen to share their thoughts. I've added both dates and the accumulated miles hiked for each reflection as a guide for readers to see where I was in my grief journey when each thought, memory, or emotion struck me.

It is difficult to paint a picture of a person's life and loss without telling stories that will make you laugh, cry, or sometimes, both. Some short background may help with context, however.

Amy and I were married on December 30, 1989, exactly one year after our engagement. We became engaged after knowing each other for only five months of a long-distance relationship and were happily married for the next thirty-two years. Amy and I were blessed with three wonderful children—our daughter, Claire, and our identical twin sons, Morgan and Carson. Our lives were filled with both challenges and triumphs. I will share many of these with you.

As you read the stories contained in this book, there is only one important thing to know: Amy is, and will always be, the *love of my life*. Cancer deprived me of her and the future we had planned, and I am broken beyond what any words can express. I am fortunate to have many family and friends to support me, but this book shares my grief journey and my search for healing.

November 10, 2022 | Miles Hiked: 28

RUN, FORREST, RUN

I AM NOT SURE WHEN I realized that Amy was going to die. The seriousness of her diagnosis was apparent from the beginning. Her medical team acted with haste to move Amy to the front of the line for scans, radiation, and chemotherapy. The location of her metastasized cancer put her at high risk of vascular compromise. Their urgency told us all we needed to know.

At some point among all of the appointments and scans, most families will inevitably ask *the question*: How long do I have? I am sure medical professionals dread this question. As our doctor relayed to us, statistics apply to groups, not individuals, and there is no way to predict outcomes in any individual case. But, as to the statistics for cases like Amy's, he estimated one year if it acted like pancreatic cancer and perhaps closer to two years if it behaved more like colon cancer.

At one of the appointments after it became apparent that it was unlikely we would ever know the origin of Amy's cancer, I pressed our doctor for an educated guess on what type of cancer it might be. He deftly sidestepped my question, but when I pressed him again, he admitted he suspected it was pancreatic cancer. Given Amy's chemotherapy regimen was textbook treatment for pancreatic cancer, this only confirmed what we had already guessed.

It was sometime after that discussion that I began to realize I might lose Amy. Whether it was five days, five weeks, five months, or five years, we likely were not going to be together for our golden years. After working so hard for so long to raise a family, help the kids through college, and get them launched into adulthood and into their respective careers, we were going to be denied the coveted time when most couples are able to notch it back a little and focus on their own lives. Whether it be travel, adventures, the joys of being a grandparent, or simply a slower pace, we were going to be denied that precious time together.

Amy of course vowed to fight on and was adamant that she wanted to be that one in a million that beat the odds. She was going to hang onto hope and let go of her fear. She was not open to any discussions of not achieving that goal. My sole objective, therefore, was to make every day the best day it could possibly be for her despite everything she was going through.

When someone you love has cancer, you find yourself with a lot of time to think, whether it is waiting for doctor appointments, slogging through chemo with them, or simply holding their hand to provide comfort as they doze in and out of sleep.

Gradually, those thoughts took form as grief. I began to grieve in anticipation of a seemingly inevitable outcome. I grieved knowing that I was likely going to lose my best friend and companion. Her spirit and her joy. Our future together. I was going to lose it all. How could I ever overcome such a monumental loss? I couldn't even imagine a life without Amy.

Like many who have walked this tortured path, I considered such thoughts selfish and inappropriate and rarely, if ever, discussed my feelings on the subject with anyone. Despite my shame for these thoughts, I slowly began to contemplate how I could heal from such a catastrophic loss. Maybe if I could just get through the first year or two, maybe I would be able to heal.

I found inspiration in the movie *Forrest Gump*. When Jenny left Forrest, his heart was broken, and he ran. He kept running from coast to coast and back again until his mind cleared, and he finally got tired and went home. Instead of running, I decided I would take up hiking. I would walk and lose myself in going from point A to point B. While doing this, I could revel in the infinite beauty of this country and reflect on those treasured and precious memories of Amy. In this way, I could share these adventures with her and perhaps, just perhaps, find healing on my journey. Amy would also have been pleased by the example this plan would provide Claire, Morgan, and Carson.

More than two months after Amy passed, I began laying plans to accomplish these goals. I registered to go on a thru-hike with REI Adventures to the Grand Staircase-Escalante National Monument in southern Utah. The trip was planned for late September when the weather is favorable in that region.

Four days and three nights in the backcountry and dark sky of Utah would require training for the distance and carrying a forty-pound backpack. As I learned more about backpacking through numerous YouTube videos of thru-hikers on the Appalachian Trail and the Pacific Crest Trails, I found myself at least excited by the opportunity, even if I felt guilt at the prospect of enjoying something without Amy.

Make plans. Do something. Keep moving forward. For me, that is the whole point. I hope it works.

November 15, 2022 | Miles Hiked: 66

FULL MOON RISING

DELTA RAE HAD IT right—there is "No Peace in Quiet." After the celebration of life was over and friends and family returned to their lives, the house Amy and I shared was very quiet. Too quiet. For the better part of twenty-eight years, our house had been the exact opposite, as it was typically a beehive of activity while we raised our three wonderful children.

From the early grade school years to the running—and driving—around of the middle and high school years, our house was rarely the quiet house. Our kids were never video game kids. They much preferred our enormous sand box and playset when they were little and outdoor sports and shenanigans as they grew older. The screeching and yelling from them and their friends was nearly a constant sound in our neighborhood.

One of the other mainstays at our household was dinner. We had always been a family that ate dinner together. Part of that was a function of the boys' diabetes. From a very early age, we had structured our lives around eating meals in order to regulate the boys' blood sugar levels and keep them on a healthy trajectory. Mealtime at the Youngquist household was rarely quiet. This was partly due to the post-meal sugar rush the boys experienced before their insulin could fully kick in and partly due to Amy's skill and insistence in extracting the day's events out of each of the kids.

Amy *loved* this time. Her ability to learn the details of her children's lives was the envy of every parent in the neighborhood. It even trickled down to our much more reserved daughter, as she literally would have to compete for food with two hungry boys and for gaps in the boys' conversation to share important aspects of her life with us.

Once on a particularly boisterous night at the dinner table, Morgan—a very tall six foot two at the time—saw fit to jump up onto his chair and moon his brother, who was sitting across the table from him. Seeing such a spectacle at an elevated height truly shocked Amy into full parent mode, and she scolded Morgan with appropriate vigor. Unfortunately, when she looked to me for reinforcement, I was of no help as I couldn't stop laughing at the absurdity of the entire episode.

Even after launching our children off to college and then onto successful careers, our house was always busy. Just the way Amy liked it. We were fortunate to have everything from kayaks to the coolest potato gun ever made to lure the kids back. Amy's talent for preparing food and her insistence on feeding them and their friends also had something to do with it.

I worry without that ever-present love and laughter from their mother that our house will digress into the quiet, sad house that no one wants to visit. The gift to build and nurture that same fun-loving atmosphere Amy created might be beyond my ability, especially as I mourn her absence. I have taken for granted the companionship, friendship, and love that has been a constant in this household. I miss it greatly and regret my complacency. There truly is "No Peace in Quiet."

November 22, 2022 | Miles Hiked: 100

FADE

IT HAS BEEN EXACTLY one month since Amy passed away, and I have had my moments. A light-hearted moment of laughter can turn into tears of sorrow in an instant. It is amazing how quickly your emotions can turn from one to another.

Walking continues to clear my head and emotions as I take in the morning sun or a flock of sand cranes flying overhead. It also brings back those precious gems of memories and moments with Amy.

Today, for some reason, I was thinking of the passing of Amy's grandmother, more affectionately referred to as Busia, slang for grandmother in Polish, by her family. We were headed to the north shore of Lake Superior for a long weekend of camping at Gooseberry Falls State Park, a hidden gem to everyone not from Minnesota. From Milwaukee, it is a bit of a drive, especially when you don't start until the afternoon. Our plan was to stop at a private campground just outside of Superior, Wisconsin, and then tackle the rest of the drive the following morning and be there in plenty of time for a full weekend at the park.

As we neared our destination, Amy got a call from her father telling her the sad news of Busia's passing. We were encouraged to continue on our journey while Amy's father and his sister made the arrangements for the burial mass and visitation the next week.

There was no moon that night after we put the kids to bed. We let the campfire burn down to embers as Amy talked and shared stories of her childhood with Busia. As the light faded, the dark sky lit up with the Milky Way in the northern woods of Wisconsin. The stars were so thick they looked like a layer of fog. We laid on the picnic table silently together just holding hands and staring up at the sky watching the Perseid meteor shower against the backdrop of the Milky Way.

Later that year as the holidays approached, Amy, her sister Mary, and our good friend Peg came up with an idea to bring a little joy to Busia's extended care facility, where she had lived the last months of her life. The three of them arranged to purchase a couple flats of mini poinsettias, got the first names of the residents on her old floor, and had the families decorate gift tags for each resident. We then loaded up the car and delivered them one evening to spread some holiday cheer.

As I finished my morning walk thinking about these memories,

I realized I don't want to ever let go of the essence of Amy. Her spirit remains an inspiration to everyone that knew her.

Amy, you'll be in my heart for all my days. I will never let you fade.

February 27, 2023 | Miles Hiked: 332

THE SENTIMENTAL TO CLUTTER RATIO

PROCRASTINATION HAS NEVER BEEN a trait that Amy or I shared. Typically, if there was an unpleasant task, like dusting the bedroom or cleaning out the storage room, we both agreed it was better just to pick a date and time and get it done. We always felt a sense of satisfaction and accomplishment after completing the task.

Clutter was a particular annoyance to Amy. The sentimental to clutter ratio was always less than one in Amy's world. Her philosophy was when in doubt, throw it out. On the top of her annoyance list was a box of keepsakes we had kept from our short dating period. Amy and I had a long-distance relationship.

She lived in Milwaukee, Wisconsin, and I lived in Springfield, Missouri. Since we met before the advent of texting and cell phones, we corresponded the old-fashioned way—letters and long-distance phone calls.

The keepsake box contained very personal and embarrassingly sappy letters from our short courtship. Amy attempted to throw it away multiple times, but I was able to fend her off. The box also contained some poetry I wrote her. It is not well known that I must have written her about a dozen poems that at the time I thought were not half bad. Unfortunately, it looks like Amy conducted a clandestine operation and was able to purge the box from our closet unnoticed.

Her disdain for clutter once caused a bit of a cold war in our marriage. During our honeymoon in Maine, we had splurged and purchased a watercolor of a coastal scene from one of the area's artists, Nancy St. Lawrence. It had hung in our bedroom in the early years of our marriage, but did not match the décor after we had moved into our house. It had been banished to storage under our bed for more than a decade. When we remodeled our bedroom, Amy was halfway to loading it in the car to be taken to Goodwill before I intercepted her. My sentimental to clutter ratio was very high for this painting. Fortunately, upon further inspection, it actually matched our new color scheme quite by accident and is now prominently displayed.

There is one task I have procrastinated on completing since Amy passed. I have been unable to even contemplate cleaning out the closet of Amy's clothes. I know there are no expectations or timelines I have to adhere to, and everyone moves at their own pace, but the thought of sorting through her clothes has been unbearable to me. At first, I told myself there was no rush. It can wait until after Thanksgiving, then her birthday, then Christmas, and then our anniversary.

Each day, however, I start fresh with the painful reminder that Amy is no longer here. I finally took the first step and purchased ten boxes in which to transfer everything. The boxes remained stacked in my bedroom for several days before I called Amy's sister Mary to peruse through and pick out anything she might want.

The day after our anniversary, I sorted and boxed the clothes. It was as painful as I had anticipated. Removing her clothes had a feeling of finality that was unwelcome. I believe if I had waited another year, I probably would have felt the same. I had hoped that upon completion I would feel some sort of satisfaction or accomplishment in moving forward. Instead, I feel sad and, just like the closet, empty.

March 6, 2023 | Miles Hiked: 386

BLUE BALLS

CHEMOTHERAPY IS A BATTLE for your soul. It will suck the life out of you while it is trying to save or extend your life. Our care team was very upfront that Amy's treatment was palliative in nature, not curative. The goal was to extend her life and improve its quality for as long as possible. Her particular chemo cocktail was very aggressive and only given to younger patients who could tolerate the toxicity of the drug combination.

Amy chose her sister Mary to walk this journey with her. I set aside my desire to walk every step with her knowing that Amy chose Mary for a very specific purpose—to provide some sassiness and attitude to her chemotherapy sessions.

Her treatment called for chemotherapy once every two weeks with a portable unit to be carried for an additional forty-six hours. Our routine would be for Amy, Mary, and me to see the doctor and review her blood work and the trend in her cancer markers. It was at this time that we would hit the doctor with our questions in rapid succession to make sure we understood her treatment plan, its side effects, and the goals. I would then walk with Amy and Mary over to the chemotherapy area and then go home to work for a few hours before they would return.

Her first few chemo treatments were pretty rough. Lots of nausea and diarrhea—or dee-arrrh-e-ah as she liked to call it. Amy subsequently came up with a plan to help her weather the treatments better both mentally and physically. One of the more annoying side effects for her was the cramping she got in her hands during the administration of one of the drugs. Her solution was to order stress balls off Amazon and bring them to chemo. When it came time for the administration of that particular drug, she would squeeze the stress balls to keep her hands from cramping. It was only when I received a sympathy card from the chemo nurses that I learned that Amy's reputation for squeezing blue balls was legendary among the nurses. I can only imagine the jokes Amy and Mary must have made to earn that reputation.

Another trick to pass the time while at chemo was for her to come up with sassy thank you notes to chemo. Modeled after Jimmy Fallon's thank you notes on Friday nights, she would come up with one liners to thank chemo for her various side effects.

- Thank you, chemo, for shit that smells worse than a trucker's at an all-night diner.

- Thank you, chemo, for giving me the taste buds of a fifth grader and ruining my love of wine.

- Thank you, chemo, for providing new stylish accessories for my wardrobe.

Amy and her sister would write out these thank yous on small Post-it notes and then crumple them up and toss them into a small garbage can to kill time during her treatment. I was even able to participate one week when I was filling in for Mary while she was out of town.

These snarky exercises helped Amy deal with the fact that she would be on chemo indefinitely. Our doctor never officially defined indefinitely, but we prodded him on the subject enough to know that this meant she would be on chemo the rest of her life. People would ask us how long Amy would be on chemo. When we answered "indefinitely" the implications rarely registered, and they would sometimes ask the same question weeks or months later.

Now, when I envision her sitting in her chair at chemo squeezing her blue balls, I burst with pride at Amy's courage and sense of humor under such daunting circumstances. I am humbled and awed by her positivity and spirit.

Keep squeezing those blue balls, Love.

March 13, 2023 | Miles Hiked: 409

POLKAFEST

AFTER AMY AND I got engaged, it became harder and harder for us to be apart. The weekend visits and Monday morning goodbyes always came and went too fast. Our mutual feelings on the matter were best summed up by a line from Harry in the classic movie *When Harry Met Sally*: ". . . when you realize you want to spend the rest of your life with somebody, you want the rest of your life to start as soon as possible."

So, we made a decision that at the time was somewhat controversial. We decided to have Amy move to Springfield, Missouri, to live with me prior to our wedding. This decision went over like a lead balloon—it was a different era, folks. When informed of the decision while out to eat at a restaurant during one of my weekend visits, we received a terse "check please, we will talk about this at home" from Amy's father Frank. Although we never officially received their blessing, they eventually accepted the fact that we had made a decision and were steadfast in following through.

The move was planned to coincide with Amy's brother Mark's wedding. I would fly up for the wedding, and then Amy and I would drive back to Missouri afterward.

Mark and Jody were married several months before us. Relatives made the approximately ninety-mile trek up I-43 from Milwaukee to Manitowoc, Wisconsin. I flew into Milwaukee in advance of the wedding and shared a room with the groom-to-be the night before.

The wedding day itself is always easy for me to remember as they had chosen my birthday to be married. My recollection of the day has dimmed over the years, but I remember following the wedding party from place to place as they had their pictures taken and arrived at the church for the ceremony. The dinner and reception were at Rose's Century Inn and dance hall located in Mishicot, Wisconsin.

This was my first wedding of a Polish family. Food and fun are second nature to them, but for this reserved Scandinavian, it was a bit of a culture shock, albeit a pleasant one. At some point in the night, the family sang me "Happy Birthday" in Polish for all to hear. Then the dancing began!

I was totally lost as Amy tried to teach me how to polka on the fly, especially since they threw sawdust on the floor to prime the dance floor for those of us with slippery soles. It was very fortunate that I did not break any of Amy's toes that night.

Two weeks later in Missouri, we received a small package in the mail addressed to both Amy and me. In it was a cassette tape from her father entitled "And a One and a Two" with a note hinting strongly that we—really, me—had better make a dramatic improvement in our polka before our wedding in just four short months.

So one weekend, we cleared the furniture out of our small apartment's living room and practiced for hours getting our polka down. By the time the wedding rolled around, we passed with flying colors. We even managed a few dramatic head flips for show.

Amy began her chemo in late September 2021. She was at a low point mentally and physically, having endured her diagnosis, a multitude of tests and scans, two weeks of radiation, and the shock of transitioning straight to chemotherapy. I was looking for a way to surround her with family to brighten her day.

As I recalled the events around our polka deficiencies, it hit me. Our kids did not know how to polka! I would invite the kids and their friends, Amy's aunt Pat and uncle Tom, and Mary and Jerry over for PolkaFest to teach them how to polka! Invitations went out and everyone loved the idea. I ordered a Polish flag off Amazon and hung it off our deck with pride. We then cleared our deck to create the dance floor and queued up our polka playlist from Spotify.

We lucked out and had a beautiful October day with a bright blue sky and moderate temperatures. I am sure our neighbors must have thought we were crazy. But it was worth it.

Amy beamed as Mary, Pat, and I taught Claire, Morgan, and Carson how to polka. Laughter rained down as we made flubs, and Amy and I recounted our own experiences teaching me to polka in our small apartment.

Amid the darkness that surrounded us, that afternoon, we chose joy.

March 20, 2023 | Miles Hiked: 437

A NEW NICKNAME, PART 1

DECEMBER HAS ALWAYS BEEN a very busy month for our family. Amy's birthday, Morgan and Carson's birthdays, Christmas Eve and Christmas Day, and of course our anniversary all fall within the month of December. As a husband, I often struggle with December trying to make each of these dates special. Fortunately, Amy would always drop some not-so-subtle hints for me so I wouldn't embarrass myself like I often did the first few years of our marriage.

Last night, our family celebrated Amy's birthday for the first time without her. It was hard. We of course went out for Mexican food because it was Amy's favorite. At our dinner, Amy's sister Mary asked each of us to remember one of the sillier Amy moments. It was nice to smile and laugh as we each recalled our special memories and forgot our grief for just an instant.

Later when I was alone again, I cried and ached to just hold her hand one more time. As my sadness set in, I recalled one particularly difficult December when Amy demonstrated for all that knew her how her positivity just could not be contained.

In the fall of 2016, Amy had been growing increasingly frustrated by a gradual but steady weight gain. As a husband, no subject is more fraught with danger than commenting on your spouse's weight, so the subject was never broached. When she brought up that it would be good for both of us to drop a few pounds and eat healthier, I thought it was a good opportunity to jump on the bandwagon to support her. In reality, I also had put on more than a few pounds from some really bad eating habits, especially at lunch.

After a couple of months, I had dropped a moderate amount of weight, but Amy had continued her gradual weight gain despite her efforts to eat healthier. She was very frustrated. It was also increasingly obvious in her physical discomfort and appearance.

We both began to worry in earnest that something serious was at work. We scheduled a doctor's appointment for her on December 11, just one day before her birthday. That morning, I went with her to the appointment for moral support.

Neither of us were surprised when the doctor was also concerned and ordered an MRI of her abdomen. Unfortunately, the available time slot was not for another couple of hours, and I had a scheduled lunch meeting. Amy insisted I attend my meeting as the golden rule in sales is that once a prospect or customer agrees to a meeting, never cancel. Too often you will be unable to reschedule, and an opportunity is lost.

That afternoon I had a knot in my stomach waiting to hear from her. I decided to drive home early so I could be there when she got home. As I pulled into the driveway, I realized that she was already home. I raced into the house and found her crying on the stairwell. The MRI had shown a fifteen-to-seventeen-inch tumor in her abdomen. This particular doctor, lacking any sort of empathy, had merely referred Amy immediately to an oncologist and handed her a brochure on ovarian cancer before sending her on her way. It was the worst birthday ever.

The following week, we met with the oncologist who had not only reviewed the MRI but had also had the forethought to order blood work to check for cancer markers in advance of our appointment. She indicated that the tumor obviously would need to come out as soon as possible because of its size and impact on the surrounding organs. She reassured us, however, that given the size of the tumor, the cancer marker should have been elevated significantly more than Amy's level. Her gut was telling her this was benign. She did her best to reassure us that this was something that might have a very positive outcome.

That made the next two weeks bearable as we waited for the date of the surgery. All of the kids were in college making their way through finals, so we held off on sharing the news with them until they had returned home. Unfortunately, there was urgency to getting the tumor removed, so Amy's surgery was scheduled on the only open time slot available, December 23, just one day before Christmas Eve.

The day arrived and we headed off to St. Luke's Hospital in Milwaukee for the surgery.

A NEW NICKNAME, PART 2

AMY'S DOCTOR INDICATED THE surgery would take about two hours. They would do a quick instant biopsy, and if it was positive for cancer, they would perform additional surgery to remove her appendix and other organs to make sure they got as much of the surrounding tissue as possible.

Then began the wait. A nurse called us after about an hour saying everything was going as planned and the doctor would meet with us after completion of the surgery. After about two and a half hours, Amy's oncologist came out. We were in the middle of the waiting area, but since it was only two days to Christmas, we were sharing the space with only one other family. Her doctor sat down and took a tissue to wipe a tear from her eye before she began her summary. Before she even uttered the first word, we knew it was bad news.

The surgery was a total success, she said. They removed seven liters of fluid from the tumor to shrink it enough to fit through the incision. A quick test on the tissue found it abnormal, meaning cancer. A more thorough biopsy would be performed that would take a few days, but this meant they proceeded with the contingency plan to clean house, so to speak. The oncologist described the procedure in detail and the hopeful conclusion that it was all removed and that she saw no evidence of additional cancer. After the official biopsy results came back, she would share with us her treatment plan moving forward. We were devastated.

The doctor told Amy everything after the surgery, but indicated that coming out of anesthesia, most patients will not remember the conversation the next day. Before we left for the night, however, Amy had a task for us. She did not want our friends and family worrying about her. She insisted we record a short video from her hospital bed to send to them to ease their minds.

> Hi, everybody. I just wanted to send a quick video out to let you know I am doing so well. I feel so well. I am very excited we are through step 1. I know we have heard that word cancer, but we believe we've got it all, and we think it's just a stage 1. Just wanted to send that out. Wanted to also wish you a very Merry Christmas, and we'll know more next week. So, love you all. Take care. Bye, bye.

(View the video at www.youtube.com/watch?v=mp_XVByyfuw)

We sent that video out to about a dozen friends and family. Amy's positivity and optimism from her hospital bed brightened everyone's night. The return messages of love and encouragement absolutely brightened ours. I never asked her if it was her added intent to have her bedside message rebound to us and give us hope and encouragement, but I've always suspected it was part of her true intention.

We agreed to meet before the doctor's rounds at 7:00 a.m. to refresh Amy's memory after the anesthesia wore off. Claire and Mary and Jerry joined us the next morning. Since Amy was now free of her fogginess, we asked if she remembered her conversation with the doctor. She did. Every last word. In that moment, Amy felt no concern for herself. She gently reached up and touched my cheek and asked me, "How are you doing? I've been worried about you." After going through the diagnosis and surgery, her only concern was for how *we* were doing.

We spent the day with her, but she insisted we return home and spend Christmas Eve with our generous neighbors, who had gracefully invited us to dinner with their family.

That night I couldn't sleep. I was worried that we would be heading down a path for which I was not prepared. Snow had been falling at a slow and steady pace since early in the evening. By 2:00 a.m., I had to do something to shift the negative thoughts that were swirling through my head. I put on a coat and grabbed a shovel to clear my driveway and distract my mind. At one point, I stopped shoveling and watched as huge snowflakes slowly drifted down on this most holy of nights. It was then I noticed Claire standing just inside the garage with a worried expression on her face. Dressed in her pajamas, a coat, and some snow boots, she came out and hugged me. We stayed there for several minutes in silence and understanding as snow fell on our heads and shoulders.

Following the surgery, Amy was discharged from the hospital. She was unable to go up and down stairs immediately after her surgery, so we setup a hospital bed in our living room. She would rehab by doing laps around the house. One side effect of the surgery and anesthesia was an exuberance of gas. At any moment she would spontaneously let out the loudest and longest belches ever known to mankind. It made for some good levity, and the relief it gave her was welcome.

By midweek, Amy was making progress in her recovery, and we were waiting for the full biopsy results. Claire and I were sitting in the living room with Amy watching television when her phone rang. It was her oncologist with the biopsy results. We braced ourselves, but the doctor was bubbly and almost giddy. She explained that the biopsy results determined that although the tissue was abnormal, it did not have the ability to metastasize. In other words, it was not technically cancer, but a phenomenon known as a borderline ovarian tumor. In her mind, we would need to continue to monitor Amy's levels for a couple of years, but no chemotherapy or radiation was warranted.

After finishing our call with the doctor, we all did a quick little jig around the living room and eagerly started to make phone calls to friends and family to share the fantastic news. Amy's optimism in the face of this crisis earned her a new nickname from me, *Ms. Positive*. She had been proven right once again.

*Note: The surgery in this reflection had no connection to Amy's cancer diagnosis five years later. The pathologies were very different. It was definitely a question we asked both our care team and our consultant with the Mayo Clinic.

April 10, 2023 | Miles Hiked: 480

AN EMPTY CHAIR

THIS PAST WEEK, MY daughter Claire has been out of town on vacation to experience the musical force that is Taylor Swift. She had a fantastic time in Dallas and enjoyed the concert immensely. On Saturday, she will be moving out and getting back to her own life. It has been a blessing to have her here with me as I transition to a different life. For the past nine months she has sacrificed her own life to first be one of Amy's handlers, and then to be mine. My wish is for her to focus on her own happiness. I will be forever grateful for her sacrifice and love.

It has been just me in the house this week, and I have found it more difficult than usual. I prepared a nice meal on Sunday and sat down to eat. There was an empty chair across from me. It hit me hard. I lost my appetite as I was overcome by grief.

Later, I forced myself to sit back down and eat my meal, but in the silence, I felt regret as I reflected on Amy's last two weeks. I find it difficult to discuss my emotions around these events. I foolishly assumed that since her cancer marker had come down so dramatically, from nearly six thousand to less than one hundred, that as long as it did not dramatically increase, we would have some warning of a trend in the wrong direction. Instead, her pain increased over a period of two months as the cancer marker increased only incrementally. I was lulled into thinking I would have more time.

Early in Amy's diagnosis, I wanted to talk about potential scenarios around her health in order to understand her wishes if her disease progressed. Amy refused to talk about such scenarios. She was adamant that she was going to be the one in a million to beat the odds and wanted to totally focus on her treatment and on remaining positive during the process.

At some point, I pressed the issue with her. It was an uncomfortable conversation. I had to know her wishes prior to any potential developments, even if they were unlikely scenarios. We finally had a very short discussion on the matter, but I was able to ascertain her preferences.

On the Monday exactly one week prior to her passing, Amy fell. I was at the local Starbucks getting her a cheese Danish when I got the call from Claire to come home ASAP. I raced home to find Amy sitting on the floor. Claire had been right next to her when her legs gave out and she fell, hurting her leg. In an abundance of caution, we felt it best to call 911 and have her transported to the hospital for an evaluation. Her platelets were low, likely from the two weeks of radiation she had just completed. She was given a blood transfusion, discharged, and sent home.

Because she had recently completed radiation for disease progression in her bones, we were not overly concerned. Amy, however, was becoming uneasy. The pain was becoming more than a minor annoyance. In the weeks prior to this incident, it had passed a threshold that caused her medical team to add morphine for her pain management at increasing doses.

On that Thursday, I was bringing Amy lunch when she asked me, "Am I dying?"

"No," I said, "we just have to get you past the effects of the radiation and the pain it is causing. Then we can get you started on your new chemotherapy regimen."

Amy was reaching out to me, and I blundered it. After months of not talking about it, she was finally ready to talk about dying, but now it was me who was not ready. I would not even concede it was a possibility.

On that Friday, Claire alerted me that Amy was slurring her speech and couldn't swallow. Given the developments earlier in the week, we thought it best to return to the emergency room. We alerted her oncologist and set out.

One day later, she made the decision to enter hospice care, and just two days after that, Amy passed away from complications of her cancer. Most of that time was under sedation per her request from our previous conversations.

I expected more time to say goodbye. There are so many things I would have liked to have said to her. I would have thanked her for the joy she brought to my life. For giving me her love, support, and wisdom throughout our lives. And so much more.

We are approaching six months without her. As I look at her empty chair, I feel numb and haunted by regret.

April 24, 2023 | Miles Hiked: 547

WHALE!

THIS WEEK, I HAVE been in Florida for our annual trip to Siesta Key with our good friends Joe and Jackie. When I first arrived and went out onto their lanai, I broke down. The lanai was one of Amy's favorite places in the world. We would often listen to music, relax, talk, and laugh with Joe and Jackie while sitting there together. Amy will be ever-present here, but her witty jibes and barbs are missed.

I started the trip by getting in some good walks and clearing my head. Oddly enough, my thoughts wandered from the sunshine of Florida back to our honeymoon in Maine.

After getting married, Amy and I were too strapped for money to take a real honeymoon. Amy started a new job right before the wedding and flew to Memphis for training just four days afterward. We pledged we would only postpone our honeymoon, not cancel it.

Two years later, we decided to travel up the coast of Maine for our belated honeymoon. Amy, because she loved whales and wanted to go whale watching, and me, because I loved the beauty of the Maine coastline.

We flew into Boston, rented a car, and drove up the coast. We had planned stops in Portland, Kennebunkport, Freeport, East Boothbay Harbor, and then planned to conclude our trip in Acadia National Park. Our goal was to relax and slow down after a very hectic first two years of marriage.

In our dating years, we would often read out loud to each other. We would find a nice comfortable place in the sun and take turns reading whatever novel struck us. For our honeymoon, we decided to continue with J. R. Tolkien's *The Return of the King*. We shared a sense of peace and contentment as we read to each other about the journey of Frodo and Sam and their friendship. Our reading would be done either basking in the sun and enjoying the cool sea breeze or to pass the time while traveling between destinations.

Late one afternoon, we lost ourselves in Kennebunkport reading and watching the local fishing and lobster vessels coming in and out of the harbor. We decided to treat ourselves to dinner that night at the yacht club in Kennebunkport. Since we weren't members, they made us wait until well after their usual crowds had left before seating us. Fortunately, they had a blue blazer to loan me so I could enter the premises! By the time we were seated, the place was mostly empty, except for the wait staff who gave us some extra attention, knowing it was our honeymoon. We both had the lobster. It wasn't served in the traditional style. The meat was deshelled and laid out on the plate in the original shape in a white wine cream sauce. Complemented with white wine, we both agreed it was the best meal either of us had ever eaten.

We traveled to East Boothbay Harbor the next day. At the time, this sleepy little artsy town was off the beaten tourist path. We decided to take a sunset cruise on a sailing yacht. There were only about a dozen people on board, and we were encouraged to bring our own wine and cheese for the adventure. We listened to the wind catching in the sails and watched one of the most golden sunsets we had ever witnessed. Amy, of course, extracted the captain's life story from him during the voyage. He and his family made their money during the summer tourist season and then sailed around the world during the offseason.

We stayed at two different bed and breakfasts outside Acadia National Park. The most memorable moment of the trip occurred here on our whale-watching excursion. Whale watching was one of Amy's lifelong goals. When we were signing up for the cruise, Amy was somewhat disappointed that we would not be taking a rubber dingy out for the excursion. She got a very odd look from the clerk when she asked if they had anything smaller than the diesel boat he described. That should have been our first clue that all was not as it seemed.

For most of my life, I have been deathly afraid of large bodies of water, so the diesel boat was more to my liking, especially since they take you about thirty miles out into the Atlantic Ocean. The next morning, we boarded the boat with about fifty other people, including the local chapter of the Audubon Society. These six or seven elderly ladies had to be helped aboard, which delayed our departure. Amy was about as excited as I'd ever seen her—until the boat got out of the harbor. When we turned out to sea, and the boat started to hit the waves in a rhythmic thump, thump, thump, her stomach began to churn.

She sent me into the interior concession area to obtain some Sprite to settle her stomach. The first thing I noticed upon entering was the smell. It was a mixture of pancakes, sausage, and vomit. I bought the soda and retreated outside to the deck for some fresh air. As we got further and further out to sea, things continued to decline. When the boat finally got to its whale-watching area and slowed down, it was readily apparent that we were little more than a big bobber—up and down, up and down, up and down.

Amy was adamant that she needed to get off the deck and into the cabin. I strongly advised her against entering the odoriferous interior, but at that point, I don't think it mattered. The entire boat of passengers was heaving up whatever breakfast they had consumed, and there was no safe haven. We noticed that families with small children were handing their kids to the elderly Audubon Society ladies. They seemed to be the only ones on board exempt from the seasickness spreading throughout the ship. It was the longest three hours of our lives. When we finally heard "Whale!" Amy was too far gone to care. I held her up to look just as the whale's fin disappeared below the waterline.

As we pulled into the harbor and prepared to dock, a crew of six, three on each side, came out and started scrubbing the sides of the boat from aft to stern to cleanse the vomit crusted on its sides. By then, everyone onboard was starting to recover. We felt a level of guilt as we gazed down at the eager faces waiting for the next cruise. The excursion company wisely kept us separated from them as we disembarked.

After recovering from our journey, we decided to roast hot dogs and make s'mores that night over a campfire. As our stomachs settled, we were able to laugh at ourselves and our fellow passengers, but we vowed never again to go whale watching that far from shore!

May 8, 2023 | Miles Hiked: 597

I LOVE MOM

WHEN IT CAME TO holidays, I was never the brightest bulb. I always struggled with what was appropriate. Was Valentine's Day more important than Sweetest Day? Did it outrank our anniversary in terms of importance and planning?

After numerous miscues, Amy sat me down and laid out her expectations. She told me I only needed to worry about four holidays from a gift and special event standpoint—her birthday, Christmas, our anniversary, and Mother's Day. I was free to ignore all the others as long as I gave these four the attention they deserved. For us, three of the four were in December, so remembering them was simple.

In the later years, we skipped the anniversary cards and just made sure we celebrated with friends or had a nice dinner. One year, after no cards had been exchanged for several years, I surprised her with a nice sentimental anniversary card. She was taken aback and started to sulk that she had not gotten me a card.

"Do you feel the same way towards me as the card says?" I asked.

Without hesitation, she said, "Yes."

"Well, then, why don't you sign it and give it back to me," I said.

She smiled, signed the card, and gave it back to me, earning me a very nice kiss to boot.

When it comes to nailing these four holidays, none of my gifts or dinners will *ever* compete with Carson's Mother's Day gift in the seventh grade. As far as Youngquist Hall of Fame moments go, it will forever be in the top five moments and will likely remain an uncontested number one.

It started innocently enough after one of the boys' diabetes clinics. At their appointment, they would get their A1C number and review the status of their diabetes management. They did not enjoy these quarterly reviews any more than we did as parents. All of us felt judged and uncomfortable after these reviews, justified or not. We would typically treat the boys to lunch afterward and let them skip the remainder of the school day as a reward for enduring them.

After the appointment that year, Carson shared that he wanted to put tape on his chest spelling out *I love Mom* with a heart shape for love, then lay out in the sun to start his tan. Evidently, he had taken a dare from one of his friends for the upcoming Mother's Day holiday. Amy gleefully helped him put the tape on, and we both went back to work and left the boys to enjoy their afternoon.

When I got home, I found Amy with Carson out on the backyard deck. Carson was very sunburned and on his chest was a distinct and pale outline of I love Mom. I could tell he was a little nervous about how clear his message stood out. Sheepishly, he told me he had fallen asleep while lying out, and the tape had done its job. We took some pictures to document this unique gift, and all of us got a good laugh out of it.

This was the gift that kept giving, however. Little did we know then, but the I love Mom lettering would be visible for almost a year! Amy was not shy about showing Carson's chest off to anyone who asked to see it, including the other mothers at the boys' baseball games.

As a catcher, Carson was viewed as a pretty tough kid, and his reputation made the other mothers skeptical about his unique gift for her. So, one night before the game started, Amy hauled him over to the stands where all the parents were seated and made Carson take off his jersey in front of the other moms. He gladly obliged, throwing them all into cheers and laughter. It made for a very raucous crowd that night.

Carson never complained about how long it lasted, but after a while, I think even Amy wished it would fade from his chest. His friends never viewed his *sunburn tattoo* negatively, because they knew Carson truly did love his mother. The only time it felt a bit awkward was when they were waiting in line at Noah's Ark, an outdoor waterpark in the Wisconsin Dells. They got a few odd looks from others in the line.

The love of Carson, Morgan, and Claire for their mother will never perish, and our family will forever smile when we remember

Carson's Mother's Day gift to Amy that year. It fully deserves the number one slot in the Youngquist Hall of Fame.

May 21, 2023 | Miles Hiked: 696

ANGRY BIRDS

TODAY WAS A BEAUTIFUL pre-spring day with a blue sky and a temperature hovering around 40 degrees. It was a good day for a hike after taking a couple of days off to help a friend move his son to Minnesota. My thoughts drifted to Amy during my trek, remembering when the kids were young.

Our first child, Claire, was a dream child. She slept through the night from the first day we brought her home. She was so low maintenance that it lulled us into thinking parenting one more child would be a relatively small adjustment.

Chaos theory presented us with a very different path in the next pregnancy.

"Oh! There are two in here," exclaimed the ultrasound technician during Amy's eight-week appointment.

After an initial period of stunned silence, Amy and I looked at each other and laughed. Even though we couldn't stop smiling for days, our thoughts quickly turned to more practical matters, like daycare, cars, and housing. Going from man-to-man coverage to zone coverage would mean a big adjustment in philosophy and expectations.

Foremost among those concerns was daycare. We realized quickly that it would make no financial sense for us to put all three kids into daycare, along with the added stress on our careers and mental health. Amy was determined to be an integral part of their development. She felt strongly that the early years would be the most critical part of their lives, and she did not want to leave anything to chance.

Amy told her employer that she would not be returning from maternity leave. I had the easy part; I could escape to my job every day. Amy would have the challenge of keeping up with three kids and the physical and mental exhaustion that entailed.

Neither Amy nor I remembered much from the first two years of the twins' lives. From the very beginning, we knew we were in for a wild ride. Unlike Claire, Morgan and Carson felt the need to be fed *exactly* every three hours. Sleeping through the night was not an option. Add to that the fact they both had colic the first nine months, and . . . well, you parents get the picture!

We would line up eight bottles with premeasured formula each night for the 8:00 p.m. and 11:00 p.m. and 2:00 a.m. and 5:00 a.m. feedings. All we had to do was add room-temperature water, shake, and feed. To get some semblance of sleep, we would both do the 8:00 p.m. and 5:00 a.m. feedings, but I would stay up and do the 11:00 p.m., and then Amy would take the 2:00 a.m. The theory was that we would both be able to get at least five hours of uninterrupted sleep. With the colic, however, this was a rare occurrence for both of us.

The one vivid memory I have of these feedings was the panic I felt while feeding one of the boys hoping and praying the other would not wake up until I finished with the other. Typically, as they neared the completion of their bottle, they would get sleepy and lose momentum eating. We could not afford delays, so we cheated with a trick to get them to wake up and finish their bottle. We pinched their heel. This usually roused them enough to finish their bottle so we could switch to the other one.

We battled exhaustion constantly during the first year. Claire continued to be that dream child by being Mom and Dad's little helper. Whenever we needed an extra hand, Claire was there to bring us an extra diaper or whatever was needed without complaint. She loved the boys dearly.

As Morgan and Carson grew older, the switch to rice cereal could not come fast enough. Our theory was that getting them to eat solid foods would reduce the quantity of food needed and thus the number of feedings. This *never* worked. Even as young men in their twenties, they continue to have second breakfast and second lunch.

One of the more memorable feedings came one Sunday morning. I was attempting to feed the twins before we went to church. Amy was getting ready upstairs, and I had both boys in their bouncy seats on the kitchen table. I was shoving rice cereal into their mouths as fast as possible, but they were particularly hungry that morning. They were extremely animated between bites and bounced precariously in their seats like angry birds waiting for their parent to feed them. As I went spoonful to spoonful between them, Amy came downstairs and saw them bouncing vigorously on the table. She just sighed, grabbed a baby spoon, and took over feeding one of them.

Needless to say, we were late for church that morning. We both looked back at those times, exhausted as we were, as some of the happiest of our lives. Innocent and pure, this memory is one of our most cherished. Miss you, Babe.

June 5, 2023 | Miles Hiked: 731

MACC

THE GAWRON FAMILY FACED many life challenges. Foremost among those was growing up in a home with a mother diagnosed with bipolar disorder. The family did an incredible job working through those challenges. I was always amazed at their ability to support each other and keep moving forward with such joy.

One impact of that challenge was Mary, Amy, and Mark's very conservative approach to finances. They got this from their father, Frank. Two of Frank's more memorable and oft repeated lines were:

- If you can't pay cash, you can't afford it.

- If Farm & Fleet doesn't have it, you don't need it.

I got an early indication of this financial conservatism when, the morning after I proposed, Amy insisted we sit down and develop a budget for how we were going to afford a wedding. Two days later, on her return trip to Milwaukee from Minneapolis, the transmission in her car, affectionately referred to as Chet Zesty, failed. It shattered our carefully crafted budget in an instant.

This financial conservatism contributed to Amy's reticence to take any vacation that involved travel, especially ones just for the two of us. She had a real fear of an unexpected health or financial crisis that could set us back. In her thought process, vacations abroad or involving air travel were an unneeded financial risk.

That is why it was so momentous when Amy finally agreed to go to the Mexican Riviera with our good friends Joe and Jackie. Our destination was the Riu Palace Mexico, an all-inclusive hotel in Playa del Carmen. We landed in Cancun and took an hour-long shuttle to the hotel.

When we arrived in our room and I connected to the wireless network, my phone blew up with incoming messages. Before I even had a chance to read any of them, Claire called via WhatsApp to inform us that Amy's mother, Judy, had passed while we were in transit.

Although she had been in poor health for many years, the news was a shock. After several calls with Amy's family, it was decided to delay the memorial three weeks to coincide with the grandkids' college breaks. That way they could all attend without the stress of making up midterm exams. Everyone assured Amy that Judy would want her to continue with her vacation. Amy did her best to stay in the moment and enjoy our trip, but I know it weighed heavily on her.

The celebration of life was a beautiful ceremony with family and friends gathering from all corners of the country. Judy was reunited with Frank, the always practical, in a niche that he had purchased as an anniversary gift to her one year.

Two months later, life was beginning to settle back down. Then one night in mid-April, Amy and I were watching a television show when Amy suddenly muted the volume. She turned toward me and gave me the big lower pouty lip. I knew something big was coming.

She said softly, "We need a dog again."

I was dumbfounded. Dakota, our first dog, had passed away in a tragic accident when he was only eighteen months old, and our beloved Scout had passed at only four years old from an unknown disease.

At the time, we had discussed and agreed that our family might not be destined to have a dog. Seven years removed from that discussion, we were now empty nesters and wanted to travel more. I mused that this was little more than a passing whim.

I knew that the pouty lip was not to be trifled with, however. So, I decided to call her bluff and reach out to all of the English Springer Spaniel—a Youngquist tradition—breeders within a 150-mile radius to see if any of them were expecting any litters in the coming months. Unfortunately, all were reserved. When I informed Amy of this, she told me that perhaps we could break the tradition and get another breed.

As I was mulling this option over, I received a call from one of the breeders. A family that had put earnest money down on one of her newborn puppies had backed out. She had a black and white male springer available immediately. If we wanted him, she was hoping we could pick him up the following weekend.

When I shared this news with Amy, I expected some hesitation given the reality of having a new puppy in the house. Instead, she said, "We have to go shopping tonight. We gave all of Scout's stuff away."

Later she asked me if I had thought about possible names for the puppy. I told her, "I was thinking we would take the first letter of each of the kids names and yours, Morgan, Amy, Carson, Claire, and name him Macc." She immediately fell in love with the name.

The following Saturday, we drove to Naperville to pick up Macc. When we arrived, our first impression was that the breeder was struggling with health issues. It made it difficult for her to care for so many dogs. The kennel was located in her basement, and she struggled to go up and down the stairs. Macc was adorable, but he also was pretty rank. Although well fed, he probably had not been bathed in quite a while. Macc, wrapped in a blue baby blanket, sat in Amy's lap all the way back to Milwaukee. As we neared home, Amy looked at me and said, "We saved him."

When we got home, we first reached out to Morgan and Carson via FaceTime to tell them the news before Carson had to be at baseball practice. When we introduced them to their new brother, we witnessed an unexpected display of raw emotion from both boys. They broke down into tears and took several minutes to compose themselves as they digested the news of their new family member.

That accomplished, we decided to wait to call Claire until after Macc received a much-needed bath. Unfortunately, within minutes we received a call from Claire. Carson had posted something on Twitter. Claire was very excited to meet Macc when she returned home from physical therapy school.

Macc adjusted well to life at the Youngquist household despite the kids coming and going from college and then jobs over the next few years. Whenever any of the kids visit, Macc goes crazy with excitement. Even the sight of a car remotely similar to Claire, Morgan, or Carson's will send him into a howling frenzy.

Macc was able to visit Amy when she entered hospice care. When he came through the door there were many people in the room with a lot of activity. Macc ignored everyone and everything and went directly to Amy's bedside and tried to crawl up onto the bed. We gave him a little lift, and he curled up between Amy's legs and rested his head on one of her legs. He remained there for quite some time seeming to understand the enormity of the situation.

Macc has been my constant companion the past few months as we hike mile after mile together. He is Amy's enduring gift to me and the kids. We haven't saved him. Macc has saved us.

June 19, 2023 | Miles Hiked: 783

BATHMAN

TONIGHT, I AM FLYING back from Florida. The flight is only three hours, but whenever I have too much time to think, sadness overtakes my thoughts. So, I pulled out my book of story ideas to see if I could distract my mind for a few hours.

My thought process reminded me of one of Amy's philosophies: Structure is good in all things, especially raising children. Since the kids outnumbered us and the twins had diabetes, this applied even more to raising Claire, Morgan, and Carson. Amy had daily schedules for the kids. Breakfast completed by 9:00 a.m. Playtime from 9:00 a.m. to 11:00 a.m., etc. Just because Amy had a schedule, however, did not mean she stifled their creativity.

At the center of their early play was one of the largest backyard sandboxes in the neighborhood. At twelve feet by ten feet with a massive quantity of sand, it allowed for a wide variety of construction and imagination that few of their friends could match.

Foremost among their sand creations was Happy Harbor, a name coined by Amy's brother Mark when, during one visit, they turned the sandbox into a seaside resort. Happy Harbor typically took more than an hour to build before they dragged the hose out to the sandbox. At this point, some sort of tragic tsunami or burst dam would wipe out the entire population of poor sleepy Happy Harbor. They would stomp, crush, and roll in the wet sand in delight at the village's fate. The backyard was always a bit soggy. I am sure our water bill was substantially more than our neighbors.

Happy Harbor always resulted in bath time for the kids to wash the sand, dirt, and mud off them before dinner or bedtime. As I observed Amy's approach with the kids, I made a conscious decision to emulate Amy's structured, but joy-filled, approach with them.

Thus, I created Bathman. When it was bath night or whenever they needed a bath, I would tell each of them to get ready for the bath by putting their dirty clothes in the hamper. While they were doing that, I would leave and close the door behind me. After I had filled the tub with water, I grabbed a bath towel and flung it over my shoulders as a cape and started loudly humming the Batman theme and ran into the room and started chasing them. "Na na na na na na na na, Bathman!"

I would let them run around squealing for a good while and would eventually catch them, then lift them over my head and proceed to dump them into the tub. Bath time in our house became a fun and tried tradition for a couple of years until they grew too old for such silliness. While it lasted, I never viewed bath time as a chore, but a fun escape from the more mundane parts of being an adult.

Bedtime, however, was always structured. Amy or I would read to the kids for fifteen to thirty minutes, depending on their level of tiredness—or ours. We would then turn out the light and say goodnight. After a while, I came up with the idea to expand the goodnight to "see you later, alligator." As time went on, we continued to build on the ritual by adding animals to the mix with the added challenge of saying them as fast as possible.

- See you later, alligator

- After a while, crocodile

- Toodaloo, kangaroo

- Hit the road, hoppy toad

- See you soon, big baboon

- Chow now, brown cow

- Hang loose, silly goose

- Say goodbye, butterfly

- Make a wish, little fish

- Do a jig, little pig

- Do a dance, red ants

- Sleep tight, little mites

Silly, I know, but they loved to hear these as their final goodnight.

I am far from a perfect father. At some point, however, you have to decide what kind of parent you want to be for your kids.

Through her example, Amy taught me how to be the father I always *wanted* and *needed* to be. Thank you, Love.

July 10, 2023 | Miles Hiked: 875

THE PORKIES

MY SEPTEMBER TRIP TO the Grand Staircase-Escalante is looming on the horizon. I received an email from my guide this week informing me they have reclassified the trip from medium-high intensity to vigorous.

After my initial shock, I calmed down and dug a little deeper. The trip hasn't changed, but feedback from this spring's participants and guides caused them to reevaluate the intensity. The trek has a total of 2,559 feet of elevation gain, which works out to an average of 853 feet per day. This is approximately the same as my recent trip to the Porcupine Wilderness Area State Park, more commonly referred to as the Porkies, in the Upper Peninsula of Michigan. This trip is a good benchmark of my preparedness for the Utah trip.

I arrived in the Porkies at around noon on Wednesday and checked-in at the ranger station to obtain my backcountry permit. The plan was to tackle the Escarpment Trail and then proceed down the North Mirror Lake Trail to Lake of the Clouds and one of the backcountry camping sites.

The buzz around the park—pun intended—was how bad the mosquitoes were this year due to the heavy snowpack and rapid spring melt. The temperature was just about 90 degrees when I reached the trailhead—a perfect match for what I might face in Utah. Because this was my first solo backcountry trip, I checked and double-checked my gear before hitting the trail.

The first mile was straight up hill through thick forest. The advanced scouting report of mosquitoes was extremely accurate. On the ascent to the first peak, they were swarming. Fortunately, I had prepared by spraying my clothes and gear with picaridin and applying a picaridin lotion to my exposed skin. Although annoying, my preparation prevented any bites.

I reached the first peak and was gassed. My pack consisted of a tent, sleeping bag, sleeping pad, portable chair, one extra set of clothes, and food and water rations. Totaled, they weighed slightly more than thirty-six pounds. My training weight was recommended to be 80 percent of the full weight, so I had been training with twenty-eight pounds. I felt every ounce of the extra eight pounds as I trudged up the hill.

I expected the trail to level off on the ridge for the remainder of the four miles that afternoon. Instead, it was a constant up and down over a series of ridges with at least four journeys down and then back up again.

The one blessing was that while I was on the top of the ridges, a strong hot wind gave me some relief from the mosquitoes trying to penetrate my defenses. By the time I arrived at my campsite for the night, I was exhausted.

My first order of business was to establish my camp on the shore of Lake of the Clouds. I pitched my tent and situated my gear for the night. Next, I needed to refill my water supply. I attempted to get to the lake by my campsite but was thwarted by about thirty feet of mud separating me from the water source. I decided to hike back to the bridge crossing the stream leading out of the lake to avoid the mud. I was able to climb down onto the structure of the bridge to refill my water bottles using my Grayl water purifier.

Unfortunately, once out of the wind, I was no match for the mosquitoes along the lake. I quickly gathered as many downed branches as I could from around the backcountry campsite and built a small fire. It provided enough smoke to keep the little vampires at bay while I prepared and ate my meal. For those interested, I used Pinnacle Foods freeze-dried Creamy Tuscan Chicken with Penne Pasta. It far exceeded my expectations for a freeze-dried meal, and I enjoyed it immensely.

As I ran out of easily accessible fuel for my fire, I hung my food, and anything scented, on the bear pole provided with each camp site and made a hasty retreat to the safety of my tent for the remainder of the evening. I can't say I really enjoyed my tent time, but the ferocity of the mosquito hatch left me no choice. In the future, I will be sure to download some audio books for entertainment when I am forced into my tent by the elements. For this trip, I just relied on my music and the park newsletter.

I decided to abandon my plans to hike twelve miles the next day on an easier trail through the deep forest. I much preferred to retrace my path on the tougher trail with elevation to more closely mimic my trip to Utah. It also had the added benefit of avoiding the mosquito hatch in the deep woods.

I did not sleep well that night, given it was my first time in the backcountry alone, but in the morning I was delighted to learn that one of the noises I had heard all night was actually a pair of wild trumpeter swans who were moving up and down the shoreline.

I broke camp at 7:00 a.m. and hydrated at the bridge, again forcing myself to drink one entire bottle of water before leaving the only water source until I reached the trailhead. As on the day before, the first mile was uphill and a grind.

As I neared the top of the first ridge, I noticed a black lab about seventy-five feet ahead of me on the trail. I was feeling encouraged that another hiker was already out and about when I noticed another larger moving black blob. I quickly realized that I had come across not dogs, but a bear and her cub.

I immediately began to sing and slowly backed down the path a dozen steps as I watched the mama and her cub continue unperturbed on their way down the hill away from me. I made a mental note to be more cautious in the future when I see movement ahead of or behind me.

About halfway back to the trailhead, I was once again exhausted from my repetitive ascents and descents. I decided to regroup and found a nice spot on Cloud Peak to rest.

As I gazed over Lake of the Clouds, I wondered what Amy would think of my grief journey. After eight months, I more often feel that I am just going through the motions and treading water than I am moving forward. I still tear up each day whenever a memory of her pops into my head or my voice cracks as I share something of her life with a friend. I miss her so much.

Make plans. Do Something. Keep moving forward. That has been my mantra as I go from day-to-day not knowing if the pain will ever subside or recede. Is it all just wasted motion? Am I avoiding my grief by walking hour after hour day after day? As I gaze at the beautiful view, I long for affirmation that I am doing the right things for myself and our kids.

I guess only time will tell. For now, I will be content with this breathtaking view and my successful trip to the Porkies. One step at a time.

July 24, 2023 | Mileage Hiked: 943

ORANGES

EVERY PARENT STARTS OUT with the hope and expectation that they will have a healthy child, free from any lifelong diseases or health complications. Fortunately, this is the case most of the time. Amy and I have been amazed, however, by the number of times our friends and relatives have had their lives impacted by lifelong illnesses or diseases. From autism to heart conditions, cerebral palsy, Noonan syndrome, eating disorders, premature births and asthma, to mental health, the list is astonishingly long in our circle.

Maybe we became hyperaware of this after fate knocked on our family's door in 2001.

It began as a common cold. Morgan, four years old at the time, caught a virus in the winter of 2001. As colds go, it was pretty routine. Rest, decongestant, recovery, and back to a normal routine. Amy, however, noticed things that often go right by me. After Morgan's cold, Amy casually mentioned that he seemed to be drinking and going to the bathroom a lot. We filed this observation away as this symptom lessened and he recovered from his cold.

A couple of months later, Morgan once again caught a cold. As he recovered, the thirst and bathroom trips began to grow exponentially. On Friday night, he would drink a glass of water, turn around and go to the bathroom, and then ask for another glass of water right afterward. We managed to get him through the night, but his thirst returned in the morning. We decided to seek his doctor's opinion on this development and were fortunate to get a Saturday morning appointment.

Our trip to the doctor was short. The nurse came in and pricked his finger to get a blood sample and a reading from a glucose monitor. It simply read "HI." His doctor came in after just a few minutes and told us in no uncertain terms to get in the car and drive directly to the children's hospital. Morgan had type 1 diabetes, and his glucose levels were dangerously high. A normal blood glucose level is between 70 and 120 mg/dl. A blood glucose meter can only generate an accurate level up to about 600 mg/dl. After that it simply reads "HI."

We engaged Amy's parents to meet us to hand off Claire and Carson. We then headed to Children's Hospital of Wisconsin. Because it was the weekend, they admitted Morgan to the hospital to get his blood sugar levels under control using insulin. They indicated we would need to participate in a diabetes education training session the following Monday and would need to stay overnight in the hospital to learn the basics until we could be trained in depth the following week.

Diabetes is a lifetime condition, and Amy and I were ignorant about this disease. Over the next few weeks we would get a crash course, but our first task was to learn how to take glucose meter readings and give insulin shots. The nurse handed us syringes, a couple bottles of saline, and a couple of oranges. She then demonstrated the proper technique to draw the insulin into the syringe and inject it into the body using the saline and oranges to practice. She told us the finger pricks for taking the glucose levels would hurt at first, but the pain would eventually fade as Morgan developed calluses on his fingertips.

We took turns practicing on the oranges. When it came time for Morgan's next insulin shot, the nurse asked us if we were comfortable enough to administer his insulin. Amy stepped forward without hesitation and gave Morgan one of his first injections. I followed when it came time for his next shot. We also used an empty practice syringe to poke ourselves just to see how it felt. The needles were so fine that neither Amy nor I could feel it.

They were able to bring Morgan's insulin levels back to the normal range that day and discharged us from the hospital Sunday afternoon. We drove to Mary's house, where Frank and Judy had taken Carson and Claire for the day to celebrate their cousin Cole's birthday. We lingered there as we shared with them everything we had learned at the hospital about Morgan's condition. We were under strict instructions to check Morgan's blood sugar every four hours until we completed our training on Monday.

It was there that Amy and I made a decision without even consulting each other. Since this was a lifelong disease, we both felt that it would be better to take his glucose levels and inject his insulin shots in front of relatives and friends so as not to stigmatize them. After the curiosity wore off, the finger pricks and shots would become just a normal part of his life. Everybody watched with curiosity as we checked his level in front of his siblings and cousins.

We ran into our first challenge that night when we arrived home and were preparing the kids for bed. Morgan needed an insulin shot. He had believed that the shots would end once we got home and was upset that he would need to continue getting them. He ran upstairs crying and hid under his bed. As we called for Morgan to come down, Carson, who had been a quiet observer to this point, planted his feet apart with his hands on his hips and yelled at us, "You leave him alone!! He doesn't want it!!"

We managed to get through that first night at home waking up every four hours to check Morgan's blood sugar. On Monday, we attended the training at Children's Hospital and began our lifelong on-the-job training.

Carson, Morgan's identical twin, was diagnosed just six months later, and we never broke stride.

As difficult as it was raising two diabetics through childhood into adolescence and adulthood, I believe how we navigated the boys' diabetes was one of our finest moments as parents. They have never let their disease stop them from accomplishing their goals. Whether it was sports, academics, or their careers in law enforcement, they have forged ahead and never let their diabetes define or limit their aspirations. Of that, we can be proud.

August 7, 2023 | Mileage Hiked: 1,015

OPERATION BRASSIERE

*This reflection is co-authored by me and Amy's sister
Mary. I enjoyed working on this particular story as the
love Amy and Mary had for each other is apparent.*

AMY HAD A MISCHIEVOUS streak, especially when it
came to her sister Mary. This probably stems from their
sharing a bedroom for most of their young lives. Mary's fortieth
birthday was a golden opportunity for Amy to prank Mary that
she couldn't pass up.

Months before Mary's birthday, Amy began scheming. She
clandestinely obtained the addresses of all Mary's friends from
her extensive address book. From the names of fellow teachers,
neighbors, friends from church, and their large book club, Amy
sent a request for everyone to send her a spare brassiere. Her

plan was to assemble as many as possible and string them up across Mary's front yard on the night of her birthday.

As the date approached, the bras began arriving via the US Postal Service. We were inundated with packages. People were not content to send just one. They often sent multiples, ranging from old worn ones to colorful new risqué styles. By the time Mary's birthday arrived, Amy had assembled approximately seventy-five for the cause.

She enlisted the help of Mary's husband Jerry to take her to Lake Geneva for a spa day and birthday dinner. This allowed Amy and her team of miscreants the opportunity to string the bras together from one end of Mary's property to the other. They even managed to cover Jerry's vintage International Harvester tractor in the front yard. The sign read: "Happy 40th Birthday from a Few of Your Supporters."

The plan worked to perfection. Amy was waiting in Mary's front yard along with her mom, Judy, and Mary's sisters-in-law, Judy, Jacque, and Jean. Amy's handy work was on glorious display, highlighted by several high wattage spotlights to be sure to draw the attention of anyone in the neighborhood.

When Mary arrived home, she was blindsided by the shenanigans and deemed it an epic prank. Mary immediately began plotting her revenge. She boxed the brassieres for future payback and even went so far as to add to the collection with several trips to Goodwill.

Amy did not like surprises. Mary also knew that Amy would get suspicious of any plotted revenge the closer Amy's fortieth birthday got. So, she planned a sneak attack in early August, months before Amy's December birthday. Her book club had been discussing assembling at the farmhouse of one of their members to celebrate the completion of a labyrinth they had built on their property. Mary scheduled a fake date for this celebration but enlisted their fellow book club members into this red herring.

Instead, Mary directed everyone to assemble at a neighbor's house several blocks away. The entire posse of scheming women proceeded to put the donated brassieres on the outside of their clothing. They then paraded through the neighborhood with the one-hundred-bra collection attached to a banner reading: "Amy Is 39 and Holding." The spectacle of all her neighbors, friends, and family, including Claire and her young friends, marching up to her house in bras caught Amy completely off-guard and she couldn't stop laughing. Amy's parents, Frank and Judy, couldn't allow the event to go undocumented, so Frank recorded the entire parade and Amy's reaction.

A party broke out as they all gathered on our deck for cocktails and snacks for the remainder of the evening to celebrate Amy's fortieth birthday a few months early.

Amy didn't need much of an excuse to dance. You can imagine the rest.

Operation Brassiere was a complete surprise and provided Mary successful retribution for Amy's initial prank more than three years prior.

As an aside, a gentleman from Lowe's was scheduled to measure for new patio doors that night. When he observed the celebration, he declared, "I've got to move into this neighborhood!"

August 21, 2023 | Miles Hiked: 1,071

MISS INDEPENDENT, PART 1

RAISING A CHILD TO be academically, socially, and financially independent is a goal of most parents. When it came to Claire, Amy and I hit the jackpot. From elementary school to adulthood, Claire displayed a self-reliance and confidence that would make any parent proud.

Part of that independence can be attributed to the demands that raising Morgan and Carson, twins with special health needs, put on Amy and me. Fair or not, Claire often got the short end of the stick when it came to our attention as we juggled Morgan and Carson's feedings, rambunctiousness, and later their medical conditions.

One morning when Claire was in the second grade, she came down to breakfast before catching the school bus and proceeded to tell us that she had a dental appointment that afternoon. She asked that we pick her up by a certain time. Afterward, she told us, we needed to take her directly from the dentist to swim club that evening.

As Claire grew older, she remained extremely organized—just like Amy—and focused on her goals. Claire was not a natural athlete, but something about swimming appealed to her, and she applied herself to the sport with vigor. She rarely missed practices at the Menomonee Falls Swim Club. It gave her structure as she balanced her wellness, social life, and academic goals. It may surprise many of you to know that Claire is the only Academic All American in our family, lettering in swimming all four years in high school and having a GPA higher than 3.6.

She breezed through high school and headed off to the University of Minnesota to pursue her goal of becoming a physical thera-pist. Of course, she had already planned her route through her undergraduate program to best position herself for that goal.

Dropping Claire off at college was one of the few moments when we were able to see her confidence and self-assurance waiver slightly. She tells us the story that after we left her in the dorm, she went to an adjoining room to introduce herself to her dormmates. She plopped herself down in their midst and admitted to not wanting to be alone. Of course, they all became the closest of friends.

Amy, sensing Claire's vulnerability at that important life milestone, wanted to call her before we were even fifteen minutes down Interstate 94. I was able to dissuade her, but Amy cried for at least the first hour of our return trip home.

Claire's hesitancy was short-lived. She absolutely thrived in college. From earning a position on the athletic training staff as a freshman, which is extremely rare, to traveling to Oregon with a group volunteering for Habitat for Humanity, she embraced the college experience. Bundled against the bitter Minnesota winter, she and a handful of friends were featured on the front page of the *St. Paul Pioneer Press* protesting athlete sexual misconduct on campus.

We never received the dreaded I'm-in-over-my-head call many parents receive at some point in their child's college experience. Claire just never needed the support and encouragement that many young people her age need to work through transitioning to adulthood—until her graduate program for physical therapy, that is.

The admissions process was stressful for Claire. After going down to the wire without being accepted to any of the dozen or so programs she had applied to, she was prepared for a gap year.

Then on a Tuesday afternoon, I received a call from Claire during a lunch meeting with a client.

"I've . . . got . . . an . . . interview . . . at . . . Western Kentucky!" she sobbed.

The interview was for *that* Friday in Bowling Green, Kentucky. Attendance was mandatory for admittance to the program, and she had just two days to juggle her midterm exams and make travel arrangements.

The plan was for me to pick her up from the Nashville airport and drive her the ninety minutes to Bowling Green for her interview the next morning. On her way to the airport, she received a notice that her flight was being delayed. Because it was the last flight out, we both suspected it would be cancelled—it was. I encouraged her to get to the airport as quickly as she could and get on stand-by for the only other flight. She made it onto that plane by the narrowest of margins.

The process involved a group interview as the prospects were ushered from area to area to learn more about the Western Kentucky PT program and talk to the various professors. As the participants gathered for the concluding statements from the staff, the phones of numerous applicants began to go off with notices of acceptance to the program—an unfortunate and mistimed miscue by a staff member.

Claire's phone was silent, but she was not deterred. Given the last-minute invitation, she figured she would be waitlisted. Every month she received an email asking her if she was still interested in the program. She went from forty-eight on the list to seven, then to three. Shortly thereafter, she received her notice that they had a position for her.

The celebration was short-lived as Claire scrambled to find living arrangements and complete her finals at the University of Minnesota.

Getting into the program would turn out to be easier than making it through.

September 4, 2023 | Miles Hiked: 1,132

MISS INDEPENDENT, PART 2

THE WESTERN KENTUCKY PT program was only in its fifth year, and the school was hyper-focused on ensuring all students passed their boards at the end of the program. Thus, they implemented a stringent grading policy. A grade of C in any class would result in academic probation, and three grades of C would result in expulsion from the program.

Claire was challenged academically right away. For Amy and me, it was a shock to receive multiple calls each week as Claire sought support. Amy was the master of problem-solving and guided Claire to seek help and tutoring early in the program. When Claire needed to stay in Bowling Green for the Thanksgiving holiday to focus on her studies, Amy did not hesitate to take Thanksgiving on the road, both to provide moral support and to give Claire some good old-fashioned home cooking.

Claire was able to stumble through the academic portion of the program and seemed to gain confidence as she transitioned to the clinical portion with rotations from Louisville, Kentucky, to Philadelphia, Pennsylvania. Those ventures are stories in themselves, so I will just say that I am not a big fan of Airbnb.

COVID hit as she was finishing her clinical in Philadelphia. COVID lockdowns struck the east coast first, as Philly became a hot spot early in the pandemic. The seriousness of the pandemic did not reach Kentucky as quickly, and her academic advisors were somewhat slow to react when her clinical rotation was cut short. Amy and I were in Florida for Carson's spring baseball trip with UW-La Crosse when Claire called and warned us that the East Coast was shutting down. After her clinical was terminated, we agreed that she should pack up and head back to Wisconsin. Our trip was also cut short as the world experienced its worst pandemic in one hundred years.

Only two hurdles remained between Claire and her goal of becoming a physical therapist. First, she needed to pass her boards, and second, she was going to need to find a job amid a pandemic.

Because the pandemic had shut everything down, Claire had ample time to study. But the date of her exam was only four months away. Claire's strength was always the clinical part of the PT program. She admitted that the academic portion was going to be difficult for her. Despite the best test prep materials, she struggled to pass her practice exams. Ever the problem-solver, she found a tutoring program to help with her preparation, and she participated in their online discussion group to glean every last morsel of advice from individuals who had already taken the exam.

Amy and I helped as much as we could, but without any personal knowledge of the source material, our assistance fell more to moral support and quizzing her on the hundreds of flash cards she had created. We would take nightly walks through the neighborhood quizzing her on the difference between dysdiadochokinesia and dysmetria and hundreds of other esoteric terms to us.

These walks were not my favorite, but Amy insisted I participate.

"She's never needed our help until now. You're going to put on your big boy pants and help her even if you don't understand a word of it!" Amy chided me.

Claire took practice test after practice test. She went so far as to time herself taking the test with a mask on to be sure to replicate the exact conditions. At the end of July 2020, Claire took her boards.

Claire has always had an uncanny ability to predict and forecast her grades. She came home neither excited by her effort, nor disappointed. For once, she had no idea how she had done but was optimistic. While she waited for her results, Claire dived into her job search.

The results were released just a week later. Claire had passed. Less than a month after that, Claire received a call from Pro-Health Care with an offer to be a physical therapist at Oconomowoc Memorial Hospital. After hanging up, Amy, Claire, and I did some celebratory dancing. She soon embarked on her career.

Because of the pandemic, Claire was deprived of a graduation ceremony, so we made sure to celebrate her accomplishments here in Wisconsin. Her family is so proud of her achievements and her fortitude in pursuing her goals. As Amy would say, "You did it, Sweetie!"

September 18, 2023 | Miles Hiked: 1,188

PICTURED ROCKS

THIS WEEK, I COMPLETED a thru-hike at Pictured Rocks National Lakeshore along Lake Superior. It was my intent to make this my first multinight hike and test my endurance carrying the full weight of a forty-pound backpack.

For me, it is much more enjoyable to hike with someone, but the pool of available friends and relatives to take a forty-two-mile multiday hike through the wilderness is small. Fortunately, my cousin Paul was available and up to the challenge. He accepted my invitation to accompany me on this journey.

Although not a hiker himself, Paul has completed multiple marathons, so we were confident he would be able to complete the four-day, three-night hike. The first challenge was procuring light weight hiking gear. He needed a tent, sleeping bag, sleeping pad, and backpack. I was able to borrow most of these items from generous neighbors—thank you, Dana and Thomas. I found a tent in the return bin at REI at a small fraction of its cost new.

A couple of nights before our trip, I set out all the items we needed on my basement floor and double-checked our gear. I charged my Garmin InReach Mini satellite GPS communicator and attached it to my bag. When everything was packed, my backpack weighed in at exactly forty pounds while Paul's weighed in at thirty-five.

The plan was for us to embark from Munising Falls on the North Country Trail heading east toward Grand Marias. We would cover approximately twelve miles each of the first three days and six miles on the final day. Total mileage was forty-two miles.

The weather was perfect with just the haze from the Canadian wildfires keeping it from being a perfect start. We were on the trail by 9:15 a.m. with a goal of making our first campsite at Mosquito River by 3:00 p.m. It seems like any hike I take the first mile is always uphill. This was no different. We anticipated the first few miles would be through the deep woods with little to see, so we set a brisk pace to eat up some of the miles. Day one was uneventful with little to note. I would have preferred the trail to be better marked with blazes, but I am not sure if the National Park Service allowed them. It created confusion from time to time as trails intersected with no clear markings.

We made Mosquito River with relative ease a little after 3:00 p.m. We set up camp after spending about fifteen minutes searching for the correct site. For some reason, site four was the only site not listed on the map. We finally came across a site with the number four scratched onto the marker by previous campers.

Mosquito River was busy. Day hikers could get to it with a relatively short two-mile hike, and the kayak companies dropped off their clients in the vicinity, making for a very busy area. After a leisurely dinner and dip in the lake, we sat up talking. We were relieved that Mosquito River did not live up to its name as there were relatively few bugs at all. We hit the sack by 9:00 p.m. with another big day ahead of us.

The forecast for day two was for showers later in the afternoon. With that in mind, we broke camp early, hoping to reach our next campsite at Pine Bluff before the rain. We realized after an hour on the trail that the showers would arrive much earlier, as we saw some ominous clouds to our west. We donned our rain gear when the showers caught up to us, but it only rained for about an hour as the trail wound its way through the canopy.

Our pace was slowed as we circumvented numerous areas of mud. All morning, we made a steady climb through the woods and were finally rewarded when the trail leveled off at the top of Pictured Rocks' majestic cliffs. The trail followed the edge of the cliff for the remainder of the morning with several spots where the trail edge literally dropped two hundred feet to Lake Superior. The views were breathtaking.

At one point, we came across a young buck with velvet on his antlers. He was making a meal of a root just off the edge of the trail. The trail went directly between the buck and a two-hundred-foot drop off. We were a little shy of trying to pass him that close to the edge of the cliff, but he refused to yield. I could have reached out and petted his nose as I slowly passed him. The root must have been a delicacy because our passing did not dissuade him from continuing his meal!

Late that morning, we reached Grand Portal Point. I can best describe this spot as a quarter-mile sandy ledge. It was beach-like, but with a two-hundred-foot drop to Lake Superior. The rain broke and it started to clear, so we pulled out our chairs and lingered for over an hour. Only one other hiker came through during that time, so we had the view all to ourselves.

Later in the afternoon, we took a break on a similar shelf near Spray Falls and met two families and their grandfather who were making a shorter trek. It was nice to share the view and stories of our journey to date. The towering cliffs morphed to elevated sand dunes as we made our next campsite, Pine Bluff, by 3:30 p.m. Paul and I were both a bit gassed, so the sandy beach near our campsite was a welcome respite to wash some of the days grime away. At this point, the beach stretched for miles.

That night, we met two families from the Cincinnati area and a couple from just east of St. Louis around the communal fire ring. We enjoyed their company. By 9:00 p.m., or hiker's midnight, we all headed off to our tents to recharge for the following day.

Day three dawned with a promise of perfect weather. We had a leisurely breakfast before we hit the trail. Since the trail hugged the shoreline of Lake Superior, Paul and I decided to walk the beach for as long as we could before rejoining the trail. We managed to hike two miles on the water's edge with just the sound of the lapping waves to keep us company before we had to rejoin the trail.

We once again decided to take extended breaks every three or four miles to rest up and hydrate. Twelve Mile Beach and Hurricane River were nice stops as the accumulated mileage began to cause fatigue. Reaching our campsite at Au Sable East around 4:00 p.m. was welcome, and we had clocked a total of thirty-six miles.

That night, we met four couples from Toronto around the communal campfire and shared our stories. Ironically, they were doing the exact same hike at the same campsites, but in the opposite direction. We turned in around 8:30 p.m. with plans to get an early start in the morning.

We broke camp around 6:45 a.m. and hit the trail. We managed to take in the early morning sun over Lake Superior as we headed east toward the dunes. Our final destination turned out to be 7.2 miles instead of six that morning. After hiking thirty-six miles, that extra 1.2 miles seemed somewhat unfair. The first mile was a grind, and we had to climb from lake level to the top of the dunes, a 350-foot ascent. We rested at the Log Chute to catch our breath for the final push. We resisted the temptation to descend the Log Chute after seeing a sign warning us that although the trip down was quick, it could take up to an hour to climb back up the dune.

With the end in sight, we hit the trail again. The trail was kind and gave us a relatively flat, wide path for several miles. We covered five miles without a break before stopping one last time to hydrate and tackle the last mile. We caught our second wind as we neared Grand Sable Visitor Center and the completion of our forty-two-mile trek.

As the parking lot came into sight, I was overwhelmed with emotion thinking about how proud Amy would be of us for completing this goal. A year ago, I would never have imagined being able to spend four days and three nights in the wilderness, let alone walking forty-two miles. I can honestly say I enjoyed this trip more than the Porkies thanks to the company of my cousin Paul and the people we met along the way.

The Grand Staircase-Escalante National Monument awaits me at the end of September. I feel prepared for the trip, but I worry about the void that will be waiting for me upon my return. I have been razor focused on training and preparing for this one event. How will I deal with the emptiness afterward?

I am going to need a break both physically and mentally after this trip. My feet certainly need to recover from walking roughly 1,200 miles since Amy passed.

I am not sure what lies ahead for me in this new life I have been forced to architect. I imagine I am going to need to continue to rely on my friends and family as I walk this journey. But I know Amy would want me to embrace the joy of this challenge and soak in the beauty of the Grand Staircase-Escalante National Monument.

Miss you every day, Love.

October 2, 2023 | Miles Hiked: 1,208

TAMBOURINE

I AM SURE MANY PEOPLE have given or received gifts from time to time that are beyond special. They are either so thoughtful or so capture the personality of the person as to cause shock and awe to the recipient.

One Christmas, Amy surprised me with such a gift. My roots to Minnesota run deep with most of my family living in the state. Growing up, my siblings and I developed very strong ties to all the failing Minnesota sports teams. Whether it was the Twins, the North Stars, or the University of Minnesota Golden Gophers, both football and hockey, our family was the epitome of the word *fan*. This included being a long-suffering Minnesota Viking fan. Please note, you cannot separate the word *long-suffering* from the words *Minnesota Viking fan*. Watching your team lose four Super Bowls during your childhood and then never making it back to the big game decade after decade makes you a pessimist at heart.

I guess it is what you are raised with during your childhood that makes those ties run deep no matter where in the country you end up living. For me, my pride in being the first graduate of the University of Minnesota in my family ran deep. I had Gopher t-shirts, sweatshirts, jerseys, beer glasses, and . . . well, you get the picture.

One year, Amy surprised me by framing a charcoal print of the Mall of the University of Minnesota campus and my degree from the Carlson School of Management. It had been gathering dust in the storage area of our basement for more than a decade. When I opened it on Christmas morning, it left me speechless. I value this gift more than any I received from Amy in our thirty-two years of marriage.

There was one gift that I gave Amy for her birthday that became *that* gift for her. I wish it were because of my thoughtfulness, but I really thought it would get a few good laughs and then be forgotten.

Amy and I love, love, love music. Amy grew up with music in her family. Her parents often listened to music, including Peter, Paul and Mary, Dan Fogelberg, James Taylor, Neil Diamond, and the list goes on and on. This love of music was passed onto each of their children.

Unfortunately for Amy and me, neither of us had a lick of musical talent. My mother played the accordion and appeared on television back in the late 1950s, but for whatever reason, her talent never manifested itself in me.

During elementary school, every student was required to learn to play an instrument. I was assigned the trombone and had a weekly music lesson. I stopped going after only two weeks. I fully expected to be reprimanded after parent-teacher conferences, but surprisingly, neither my parents nor the teacher ever spoke to me about it. I guess they knew a lost cause when they saw one.

Amy was similarly devoid of musical talent. What she lacked in actual talent, she more than made up for with passion and enthusiasm for the various music she loved. One time after a particularly rough semester in college, Amy celebrated the end of finals by playing the music in her car so loud that it took the police more than a mile with sirens and loud speaker to pull her over. In our kitchen, a sign reading "This Kitchen Is for Dancing" has been prominently displayed as long as I can remember.

We joked for many years that if we only had any musical ability at all we would be famous. So one year, I came up with the idea to give Amy a tambourine for her birthday. It combined her love of music and dancing. Let's be honest, musically, it needs only a minuscule level of skill.

Her look of shock and pure joy when she opened her present was priceless. It was love at first sight. From that point forward, Amy would bring her tambourine to neighborhood gatherings and dance to the music along with her tambourine. If she forgot it, she would send one of the kids off to retrieve it for her. It was not uncommon to see Amy dancing and playing it on top of tables as the evening progressed. Our neighbors Kaye, Louann, Carol, and Diane were often up there with her.

I never envisioned that this one gift would capture Amy's personality and spirit so completely. It became legend in our neighborhood. Rock on, Amy!

October 16, 2023 | Miles Hiked: 1,263

AUTUMN

OCTOBER HAS ALWAYS BEEN a special month for Amy and me. Our long-distance relationship grew quickly after my initial September visit, and I returned the following month. We took a hike in the Southern Kettle Moraine State Forest and carved pumpkins.

The pumpkin carving became an annual tradition. Amy and I would put in George Winston's album *Autumn* and do our best to carve creative and unique designs. When Amy was too sick to participate in 2021 because of chemotherapy, Claire stepped in and carved with me.

It was fitting then that Halloween in our neighborhood was always a celebration that Amy enjoyed immensely. Sussex was one of the first communities in the Milwaukee area to return to nighttime trick-or-treating. Our neighborhood consists of over five hundred homes, most filled with young children in the early years. Practically every home would cover their lampposts with a plastic pumpkin mold. Visitors would often joke that it was part of the homeowner's association bylaws that you had to display one. If you did not have one, it was the exception. It makes for a festival type atmosphere as the community celebrates on the last Saturday night before Halloween.

Besides the array of costumes, neighbors would decorate floats with themes ranging from Disco Inferno—complete with a mirrored disco ball—to hay rides and even a Shaggy and Scooby Doo themed dune buggy. They would drive through the neighborhood to cheers and shouts.

Friends and neighbors would gather around fire pits in the driveway and hand out candy. In the early years, the number of trick-or-treaters would fall somewhere between 250 and 300 revelers. One year, I talked to a new resident of the subdivision about the massive number of trick-or-treaters and advised them to stock up on the candy. They accepted my advice with a polite nod but admitted later they had to make a candy run to the nearby Walgreens for additional supplies.

Amy enjoyed working on the costumes for each of the kids, but her creativity always seemed to be more focused on Claire. She dressed her as an angel, a skunk, Barney, a rock star, and an Eskimo. Her pièce de résistance, however, was when she dressed Claire as a picnic table, complete with grapes, hot dogs, mustard and ketchup bottles, plates and utensils, and a giant ant crawling up the tablecloth.

Claire was especially mortified by the picnic table costume but was cajoled by her mother to don it two separate years. The only benefit to Claire was that many homes gave her extra candy for her creativity and originality!

When the kids were younger, Amy's parents always enjoyed joining us and the neighbors to give out the candy while we escorted the kids on their candy route. As the neighborhood kids grew older and some would trick-or-treat without costumes, Amy would always challenge them to declare their costume to get their candy. Although this annoyed many of these teenagers, they would often offer up some witty replies, and she would always reward them with a couple pieces of candy.

One year, our friends Kasey, Louann, Carol, and Kay helped launch a new tradition, Spooky Sussex. This event is typically held a couple of weeks before Halloween and features hay rides, warm cider, games, and a spooky trail through the woods at the Sussex Village Park. The spooky trail features multiple themed candy stops for the kids. The first year of the event they all donned animal themed hats, but subsequent years got more elaborate with a witch-themed stop and then the following year a stop themed from the movie *Despicable Me*. They recruited the Village of Sussex attorney to dress as Gru, and they decked themselves as his minions. It was a smashing success thanks in part to Gru stealing the show with an epic performance that night.

As we near the one-year mark since Amy's passing, I want to remind everyone of Amy's love for autumn. She would not want us to dwell on this occasion with melancholy and sorrow, but to embrace it with joviality and joy!

October 24, 2023 | Miles Hiked: 1,296

THE UNSPOKEN EULOGY

The following is a eulogy prepared by our very, very good friends Joe and Jackie. At Amy's celebration of life, Claire, Morgan, Carson, Mary, and I each prepared a eulogy. We were unaware that Joe and Jackie had prepared to speak as well. Today marks one year since our family's loss. We thought this would be the perfect time to share their thoughts.

JOE:

I'm Joe, and this is my wife, Jackie. We wanted to offer up a few memories.

Jackie said to me the problem in talking about Amy is not about where to begin but where to end. There are so many stories. It is hard to choose just a few. But we will try.

Now, I can't quite recall when I first heard anyone refer to her as Miss Amy. But it was so apt. Miss Amy. Just like a southern belle. So sweet, so kind, so genteel. And she was from the south. Just a Polish belle from the south side of Milwaukee.

JACKIE:

There were two kinds of people in Amy's world: family and friends. If you weren't the former, you were the latter. But only for ten minutes. You could be a neighbor-friend, a work-friend, or a new friend from the next table over. Give Amy ten minutes, and you would feel like family.

Some of you may know us as Mark and Amy's camping friends; this was particularly fortunate for us during the early days of the pandemic, as camping was one of the few things we could do together. Amy was a fabulous cook, and camp cooking was a particular gift. She spoiled us with her tomato bacon bread and her breakfast burritos over morning campfires as we did our best not to burn the bacon while turning her on to the wonders of camp coffee, spiked with a little Baileys. Yes, we were definitely a bad influence.

JOE:

I first met Mark over thirty years ago at work. It wasn't long before I got to know Amy as well and discovered that we all shared a love of games, especially board games and cards.

I learned early on that Amy cared more about the enjoyment of the game, and the time we spent together as friends, than about who won. There were more than a few times that Mark and I might be a touch too competitive, and she would remind us to "just get over yourselves."

Now, Jackie would be the first to tell you that she is not much of a card player. But she loved being Amy's partner in the card game of 500. Amy was incredibly patient as Jackie never really learned the nuances of the game, and instead taught her to "go for it," usually with excellent results. "I'm feeling edgy, girlfriend" was her refrain.

You can't speak of the Youngquist love of games without talking of baseball. There can be no question that is the dominant game in the Youngquist household.

The stories of the boys' baseball travels are legion, cheered on by their even more sports savvy sister, a proud dad, and a loving mom who was always more concerned with their sportsmanship and their effort than she ever worried about wins and losses or personal accolades. Amy's cheers from the stands of "Just do your best, Buddy" were the words the boys likely heard most often.

Amy also loved the beauty of baseball; she understood its pastoral elegance. During baseball season, she would fall asleep in bed watching a game, any game, with Mark next to her gently rubbing her arm.

Amy has always been the best person in any room, in any gathering that we've ever been part of. Her lifelong embrace of joy was part of what made her so special. Like many of you, we wear the bracelet that reminds us every day to Choose Joy, to be grateful for every blessing.

JACKIE:

But if we were to make a second bracelet for Amy, we think it would be Choose Kindness. In a world where so many people choose to assume the worst about each other, Amy encourages us to assume the best. To not presume malintent. To have empathy for one another. To be kind.

Amy always put herself in the shoes of her fellow human being. If some stranger was particularly nasty or rude, and we might be tempted to respond in kind, Amy would remind us that we could not know what particular hardships that person might be going through and would encourage us to be understanding. To be kind. To avoid judging people.

Amy could make very funny and irreverent observations about people. But it was never cruel or cutting. She somehow found a way to share her thoughts without judgment. If she observed a young lady who had chosen to dress in a way that might create the wrong impression, Amy might say something like "Ooh, what an interesting outfit," or "I wonder what she was thinking when she got dressed this morning?" or "Where was her mother before she went out the door?" In such a situation, Amy's instinct was a mother's concern, not a stranger's contempt.

JOE:

Amy made everyone around her better just by being in her presence. We will never be able to match her commitment to joy or her inimitable kindness. All we can do is to try to do one thing every day to be just a little bit more like Amy. And if we all do that, the world will be just a little bit better place.

November 6, 2023 | Miles Hiked: 1,320

GRAND STAIRCASE-ESCALANTE NATIONAL MONUMENT— BRYCE CANYON

MY TRIP TO GRAND Staircase-Escalante National Monument has come and gone. I have returned safely—more on that later—and I had a fantastic experience.

Losing Amy was unimaginable to me two short years ago. Then her cancer diagnosis and her passing only fourteen short months later turned my life upside down. Amy would not want me to dwell in my grief and sorrow. She would want me to embrace life with joy and love. At one point, she chided me on dwelling in a negative space. She indicated Claire, Morgan, and Carson would need me more than ever. I have found it to be the opposite. I have needed *them* more than ever. It is a shock to the system when roles are suddenly reversed and you find yourself more reliant on your children than they are on you.

I began to contemplate how I could possibly heal from the loss of the love of my life. I decided if I did not add structure to my life, my road forward would be dark. Unfortunately, I no longer felt any passion for my career as a sales professional and knew that if I relied on work, it would just lead to frustration and disappointment.

So, I pulled a Forrest Gump. Instead of running, I would hike. Walking every day would make me physically tired and provide structure for each day. But I still needed a goal. Like my friend Sue, who is walking the Camino de Santiago, I needed something big that I had never done before to give me focus and motivation. Thus, I decided to go on a thru-hike with REI Adventures.

From a multitude of offerings, I selected a trip to a part of the country I had never seen before and that was truly rugged and remote. The four-day trip to Grand Staircase-Escalante was a perfect fit for my goal. It consisted of an eighteen-mile route through the last part of the continental United States to be mapped. The activity level was rated medium/high in terms of difficulty and would challenge me physically. REI later upgraded its categorization to *vigorous*.

As the trip approached, I felt confident that my training regimen of hiking forty-two miles per week with a backpack at 80 percent of the trip's anticipated weight would be more than sufficient to prepare me. To a certain degree, I thought I had overtrained.

I arrived in Las Vegas on Wednesday, September 20 to enjoy a couple of days in Vegas before embarking on the trip. I rode the roller coaster at New York-New York in Amy's honor. It was Amy's highlight from our previous trip to Vegas for a work conference some twenty years earlier. On a lark, I found a Texas Hold'em tournament at one of the casinos with a $60 buy-in to see how I would fare. I finished second with a modest payout that put me in a good mood for the start of the trip the next morning.

On Friday, we marshalled at the hotel to meet our guides Patrick and Dan from REI Adventures. The other backpackers were Alice, Richa, and a mother-daughter duo, Kathy and Alex. We soon set off on the five-hour drive to Bryce Canyon National Park. We would take a warmup three-mile day hike through its distinctive hoodoos, towers, and spires that appear as forests of rock. We arrived in the park shortly after lunch. The infamous formations were awe-inspiring, even more so after we hiked to the bottom of the canyon and gazed skyward. The unique red rocks were stunningly beautiful and a perfect contrast to the crystal blue sky. Although our detour only lasted a few hours, I highly recommend adding Bryce Canyon to anyone's bucket list.

That night, we camped at nearby Kodachrome Basin State Park. It got dark soon after we arrived, but we were able to set up our tents and get situated while Patrick and Dan made us a delicious dinner. Later we did a gear shakedown, and I decided to jettison some optional items from my pack to reduce weight. We lingered around the campfire until the conversations began to lag, then we all headed to our tent for the night.

I had a restless night in the tent as I was anxious to get on the trail the next day. I gave up on sleep around 4:00 a.m. and opted to take in the dark sky of Utah for a couple hours. Overnight after consulting with our guides and discussions with her daughter, Kathy decided that the hike would be too much of a physical challenge for her to complete. I appreciated her honest self-assessment as I began to contemplate my own readiness.

As we approached the trailhead, the terrain was formidable. It consisted of desert with rolling rock formations as far as the eye could see. It was apparent that the hike was going to involve constant ascents and descents over the stark rocky landscape. As the oldest remaining hiker, I questioned my own fitness despite my extensive training.

Our guides explained to us that the name Grand Staircase refers to topographic benches and cliffs that step progressively up in elevation from south to north. The risers correspond to the benches, terraces, or plateaus in the staircase. The bottom of the staircase ends at the highest bench of the Grand Canyon in Arizona. Essentially, from the top of the monument, geological steps descend into the Grand Canyon. Each of the five *steps* has been eroded, revealing cliffs of distinctive color. The Grand Canyon has the oldest sedimentary layers, then as you move toward Bryce Canyon you see the newest.

We reached the trailhead, and I stiffened my resolve to complete the hike. The plan was for Patrick to lead us at a relaxed pace fully loaded with our gear until Dan could drop off the van at the other end of the trail, get a shuttle ride back to the trailhead, and double-time it to catch up to us on the trail shortly after midday.

After a brief photo before the signage of the Boulder Mail Trail, we embarked on our adventure.

November 13, 2023 | Miles Hiked: 1,343

GRAND STAIRCASE-ESCALANTE NATIONAL MONUMENT— DEATH HOLLOW

WE DEPARTED THE BOULDER Mail trailhead shortly before 10:30 a.m. It is an old mail route between Boulder and Escalante. The trail was carved out of the wilderness by mules who would make the daily trip. The first telegraph line between the two cities is still partially intact, and the route often intersects with the old wire that still hangs like a thread from the past along the trail.

Patrick took the lead, and I chose to hang in the back as the caboose for most of the morning. About midday, we stopped for an extended lunch along Sand Creek to let Dan catch up with our group. We encountered three individual hikers at various points that morning all headed in the opposite direction. As we prepared to resume our trek, Dan finally came within radio range. We continued up a lengthy incline and were able to visually spot Dan as he climbed to catch the group.

Reunited at last, Patrick picked up the pace, and we set out for our next campsite at the bottom of Death Hollow, along the similarly named Death Hollow Creek. Most of the trail traversed the characteristic arid slickrock, a barren, highly smoothed, and rounded bedrock sculpted primarily by wind. Unlike its name, slickrock provides excellent traction when dry.

Thanks to my conditioning, I was doing well with the numerous ascents and descents. We reached Death Hollow in the afternoon. From the top, we saw the descent to our campsite would follow a steep, exposed, and narrow path down 800 to 900 feet to the creek bed below. I am sure everyone in the group had some trepidation about the path forward, but we all kept our thoughts to ourselves.

Dan chimed in with some quick advice. "Nose over toes. Trust your gear! Don't walk with your weight on your heel."

Patrick reiterated, "If anyone gets nervous or anything, you can always just stop and sit down and take your backpack off."

The group cautiously descended the north face of Death Hollow. The long descent was arduous as your toes bore most of the weight on the steep decline. About two thirds of the way down,

Patrick called for a water break and attended to some developing blisters amongst the group.

With our campsite in view just another 150 to 200 feet down, we took to the trail again. As always, Patrick was leading. He was followed by Alice, me, Alex, Richa, and Dan. The trail changed to a mix of slickrock and sandstone that switchbacked its way down the remaining cliff face.

As I was taking a step, a rock suddenly dislodged beneath my right foot. Everything after that happened in slow motion.

The dislodged rock immediately created a mini avalanche of rock and sand that engulfed my body. I fell into this mini funnel shaped landslide. As I hit the ground, I distinctly recall thinking, "OK. I fell, but that wasn't too bad. I don't think I'm hurt." It was then that my backpack followed gravity's path down the cliff face with me still attached.

Alex told me later that it cartwheeled me over and down the incline. My mind processed this all in an instant. I thought that if I were to continue falling, I would gain speed and surely break bones as I careened down the cliff. At that instant, a small shrub appeared before my face. I knew that grabbing the thorny bugger would hurt like heck, but I was unsure if there would be another opportunity, especially as I gained speed. I reached out with both arms to grab it not caring about the pain or scrapes I would receive. As I seized the shrub, I worried that I would just pull it out of the ground and continue my fall. Fortunately, my guardian angel—my love, Amy—fortified the shrub, and it stopped the 250-plus-pound mass of me and my backpack from tumbling down the slope further.

As I came to a stop, it was quiet.

Then a soft voice called out to me. Alex said, "Mark. . . don't . . . move."

I assessed the situation. My backpack had slid up my body and was partially over my head. As I looked down below me, I saw Patrick scrambling to approach from below to help stabilize me. Beyond him was nothing but bare rock between me and the bottom of Death Hollow a hundred feet or so below.

The rest remains a bit of a blur as they got me back to the path and cleaned up minor scrapes and some limited bleeding. I do remember Dan, who is a bit of a storyteller, saying to the group, "When things like this happen, its crazy scary, but tomorrow or a week from now this is going to be the story of a lifetime!"

I appreciated his effort to calm me and the rest of the group down so that we could continue our descent to the bottom of Death Hollow. We would have time to reflect on events later. We completed our descent and waded down Death Hollow Creek about a hundred feet to avoid the rampant poison ivy overtaking the path.

We made camp along the creek with towering cliffs on both sides. At the water's edge, a large, majestic pine held onto the cliff face still upright but with half of its trunk hanging out over the creek with no support beneath it.

Dan and Patrick focused on cooking dinner and filtering water for the next day's hike, leaving Alex, Richa, Alice, and me free to decompress along the creek bed. The light began to fade as we were sandwiched between the steep walls of the hollow. Fortunately, a bright moon soon began to cast a subdued light that reflected off the hollow's walls.

As night descended, the temperature began to drop. The group lingered as the stars came out, and everyone shared stories from their lives. One by one, we drifted off to our tents to recharge after a big day on the trail. A universal truth about backpacking is that after a full day on the trail, there is no shame in hitting your sleeping bag by hiker's midnight (9:00 p.m.).

We awoke to a chill in the air the next morning. Dan and Patrick were already up heating water for the coffee and preparing breakfast for the group. I had avoided going back up the trail the day before, but this morning, I wandered up the trail to get a look at the site of my close call. As I stood looking up the cliff face we had descended the day before, my heart skipped a beat or two.

The slope was steep, and I surely would have continued to gain speed in my descent. What caught my attention, however, was that the slope suddenly stopped and dropped straight down to the floor of the hollow. Although I had a hard time determining how far the drop was from a distance or where exactly my fall occurred, it was apparent that I would have had serious life-threatening injuries. The shrub probably saved my life. Patrick had indicated the night before that a rescue at the bottom of Death Hollow likely would have taken ten to twelve hours.

I suspect I know how Death Hollow got its name. I wandered back to camp for breakfast sobered by my close call and thankful for that shrub. Dan later joked that it had been growing there for ten or twenty years just for me to grab in a moment of desperate need. I find that a comforting thought.

In middle school on a dare from a classmate, Carson got a sunburn tattoo for Mother's Day. It lasted more than a year, and Amy never hesitated to have him show it off.

Members of the Wild Turkeys Book Club gathered for Operation Brassiere to exact revenge after Amy's prank on her sister a few years earlier.

After a very tough first three months of chemo, our family gathered to show our love and support for Amy. At PolkaFest, Amy, her sister Mary, and I helped teach our kids how to polka.

Macc came into our lives just five years before Amy's cancer diagnosis. He provided many moments of levity and love.

Macc was able to say goodbye to Amy. When he entered her hospice room, he went directly to her and crawled up on the bed to snuggle with her one last time.

Despite undergoing chemotherapy just a few days earlier, Amy insisted on celebrating with Morgan as he was awarded the Medal of Valor by the Madison Police Department. Her heart burst with pride as all three of her children gathered for the occasion.

Amy loved to cook. She made dinner time fun and entertaining
and always managed to squeeze every last detail from
Claire, Morgan, and Carson about their day.

We took Christmas dinner on the road in 2021 to visit my parents in their
assisted living facility. In Amy's world, everyone was part of the process.

Amy and I always looked forward to our annual journey to Florida with our dear friends Joe and Jackie. There was never a shortage of funny and sometimes irreverent conversations that made us all laugh.

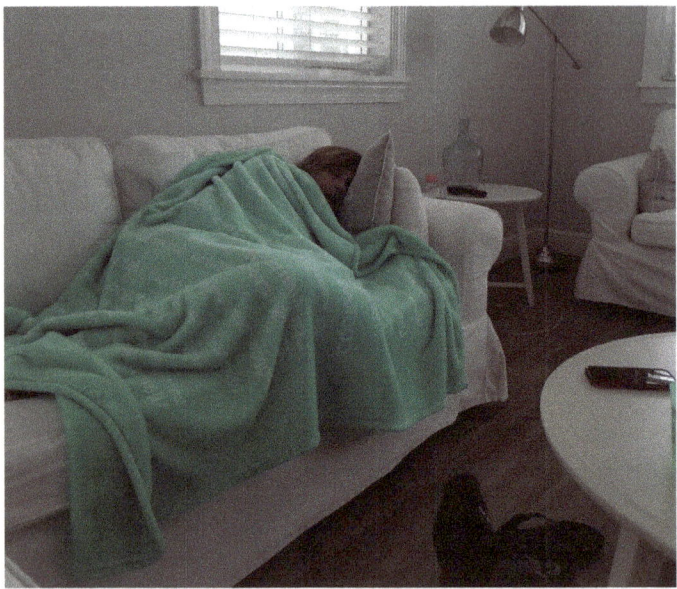

Amy taking an afternoon nap in Islamorada, Florida. I stayed by her side and contemplated our future during these incredibly difficult times.

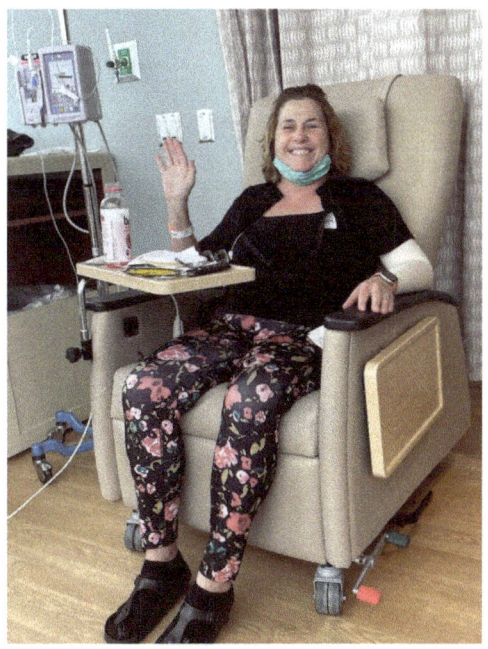

When Amy said she wanted to find joy on her cancer journey, she meant it. She always looked on the bright side of life.

Claire dressed as a picnic table for Halloween. Amy's creativity always found a home in Claire's costumes. She is pictured here with her grandparents, Frank and Judy.

Valentine's Day at the Kettle Moraine Curling Club. Amy loved curling, not for the games, but for the people she met. We consider the KMCC part of our extended family.

Amy's work for Northwestern Mutual was challenging but came with some perks—like working from home on our deck on a nice summer day.

Amy and me at a wedding for a relative in Minnesota. Of course she spent some time on the dance floor.

We helped Claire get situated for her last rotation in physical therapy school in Philadelphia.

After losing Amy, I pulled a Forrest Gump. Instead of running, I hiked. REI Adventures took a group of four of us into the Grand Staircase-Escalante National Monument in Utah. Here we are at the start of the Boulder Mail Trail.

This was the site of my close call at the infamous Death Hollow shortly before descending 900 feet to the floor of the canyon.

A natural bridge on Maime Creek. The bottomless pool pictured is just on the other side of the rock structure.

Our final ascent on the Boulder Mail Trail before descending into the town of Escalante, Utah, to conclude my adventure.

Amy and I would often read out loud to each other when we travelled. Here Amy is reading *The Return of the King* from J. R. Tolkien's the Lord of the Ring series while on our honeymoon in Maine.

A post whale-watching dinner by the campfire on our honeymoon in Maine.

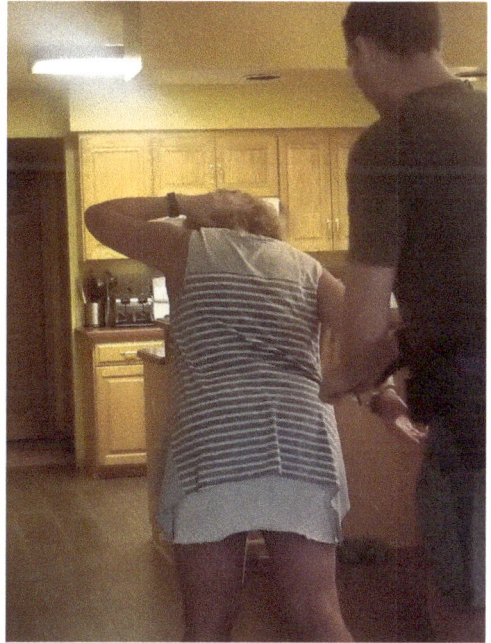

Morgan practicing handcuffing his mother for the Madison police academy. Amy was a willing test subject for the boys' techniques.

Jackie and Amy at the Siesta Key Oyster Bar—one of our favorite spots for dinner after a long day on the beach.

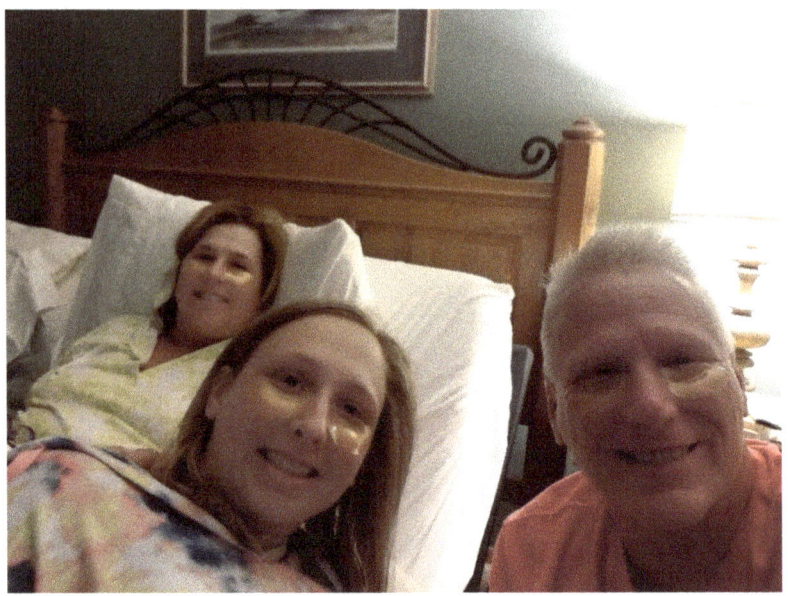

During Amy's illness, we would relax with eye masks to keep Amy company in the evenings. She rested and typically watched a baseball game.

Amy loved to stand up paddle board. We would spend afternoons on Beaver Lake near Chenequa, Wisconsin.

November 20, 2023 | Miles Hiked: 1,406

GRAND STAIRCASE-ESCALANTE NATIONAL MONUMENT— MAMIE CREEK

AFTER A LEISURELY BREAKFAST, our plan was to hike about a mile and a half down Death Hollow Creek before beginning our ascent out of Death Hollow. We donned our water shoes and set off on our morning expedition.

Patrick had advised us to follow in single file using the exact path of the hiker in front of us. We should use our trekking poles to explore exactly where we wanted to take our next step. After the first hiker, sediment would make it difficult to see the creek bottom, and he did not want any of us to twist an ankle or take a header into deeper water. It was a chilly morning, and the water was numbing, especially while we were still in the shade of the hollow.

The walk in the creek was slow and methodical, but the views of the canyon walls as we wound our way down the creek were beautiful. I should mention that the reason this creek walk was necessary was that the hiking path was totally overrun by poison ivy. It was already changing to fall colors, but that did not make it any less troublesome.

After about an hour and a half, we took a break and changed back to our hiking shoes for the long and difficult ascent out of Death Hollow. We bumped into another hiker who had plans to continue to hike up Death Hollow Creek some twelve miles. As he left, he half-joked for us to remember we saw Trevor from Texas in case he went missing.

Patrick was hoping to get to our next campsite on Mamie Creek in the early afternoon so that we could take a day hike up the creek to a natural bridge. The ascent was long and grueling on the exposed slickrock. I stuck to my plan to go slow and steady to conserve energy for the inevitable ascents and descents throughout the rest of the day's hike. I lagged behind, but do not believe I held the group up since we took more than an hour to hike out of Death Hollow.

The trail was relatively tame for the next two miles. We made good time toward our next campsite. In the early afternoon, we began our descent to Mamie Creek. It was a significant loss in elevation, but not nearly as steep as Death Hollow. We made camp without the drama from the previous day. As the four of us set up our tents and took a break, Dan and Patrick once again focused on setting out lunch and filtering water.

After eating a leisurely lunch, the group grabbed a water bottle and headed up Mamie Creek, without gear, toward a natural bridge. The creek was dry with the occasional pocket of water. At one of these pockets, we saw a small snake attempting to exit from the water up a nearly vertical incline. The snake made progress and we were confident it would make it out, so we continued up Mamie Creek. After about forty-five minutes, we reached the natural bridge.

As you passed under the bridge, the water emptied out into a larger area. I imagine at one time it created a medium-sized pool, but currently there was only a fifteen-by-thirty-foot pool of brown water. Patrick informed us that he has brought many expeditions to this natural bridge and swam in this pool. No one has yet been able to touch bottom he told us. As we explored the area and took pictures, discussion turned to who, if anyone, was going to jump into the pool.

Alice boldly declared she was going to do it and carefully made her way to the edge. Patrick gave instructions to jump to the middle of the pool where there was no apparent bottom. After a brief pause, Alice jumped in. She swam back to the edge and made her way out of the water. She declared the water was shockingly cold given the desert environment. Alice's bravery broke the ice, and Dan was the next one to take the leap.

I told the group, "I wouldn't jump in that pool for a million dollars." My statement did little to dissuade anyone in the group and they all began to take turns. Finally, Patrick, the last holdout, got ready to jump in. I decided Amy would be extremely disappointed in me if I sat this out, so I took off my shirt and made my way to the edge of the pool. As my fellow hikers gave me encouragement, I jumped in. I wasn't brave enough to go very deep. I resurfaced and quickly made my way out. It was very refreshing to rinse away three days of trail dust. Patrick and Dan returned to the water and tried to touch the bottom but were again unsuccessful. Given the darkness of the pool, I give them credit for even trying.

The group lingered near the pool and basked in the sun to dry off. I was lost in my own thoughts as the sun continued its journey across the crystal blue sky. Finally, Patrick gave the signal that we needed to return to camp. One by one, we climbed through the natural bridge for the return hike. I was the last one through. I gave a final look back, whispered my nightly missive to Amy, "I miss you, Love of My Life," and then turned to leave.

November 27, 2023 | Miles Hiked: 1,425

GRAND STAIRCASE-ESCALANTE NATIONAL MONUMENT—ESCALANTE

THAT NIGHT, WE HAD a leisurely dinner in our camp on the banks of a nearly dry Mamie Creek bed. Everyone was very relaxed as we talked about the day's hike and the plan for our final trek to Escalante the next day.

Patrick outlined the plan for the morning. It would be the longest stretch of trail, at approximately seven miles, with numerous ascents and descents. We would need to be on the trail between

6:00 a.m. and 6:30 a.m., which meant we would be starting the day hiking in the dark. He said that everyone should be up with their coffee and start to break camp by 5:30 a.m. They would have breakfast ready for us, but we would need to stay on task to make our goal of being in Escalante for lunch followed by the drive back to Las Vegas.

As darkness descended, a bright moon lit up the surrounding hills. Dan was nice enough to show me the nighttime feature on my Google Pixel 7 Pro. I experimented with it as the stars began to come out. He told me to set my phone right outside my tent and that anytime I woke up, I should just reach out of the tent and take a picture. The exposure default was set for four minutes. The moon was so bright that I would have to wait until it set to get the full star-filled sky, but even with the additional light from the moon, it took some awesome pictures.

I was very restless and found it difficult to sleep. I managed to take several photos but tossed and turned most of the night. Around 5:00 a.m., I just gave up and got up. I walked down the trail to get away from camp and experimented with my camera. I was fortunate to catch a few meteors streaking across the sky. You can see some of the pictures and videos at www.youtube. com/watch?v=eBzEJmZfx30. Patrick and Dan were up and moving to cook breakfast and warm water for coffee.

I began to break down my tent and pack my backpack. After breakfast, I offered to help others break camp, but everyone seemed to be on task. We hit the trail on time and began our ascent in the dark. Headlamps gave us light during the early part of our journey, but the sun began to light up the surrounding hills and we soon put them away. We paused at the top of our ascent about forty-five minutes later to watch the sunrise.

After about ten minutes, we were back on the trail, and Patrick set a steady pace as we made our way toward Escalante. On one of the water breaks, he indicated we had one long ascent remaining before we descended toward the trailhead and then to our van. We followed the now familiar cairns up a long hill of predominantly slickrock and again passed under the old telegraph line. After another water break toward the top of the hill, we continued on and were finally rewarded with a view of Escalante in the distance. Our descent would be slow and methodical as we wound our way down into the valley and through another canyon along Pine Creek.

After walking over 1,400 miles by the conclusion of this trip, my body was holding up fairly well. My only complaint was that the muscle strain that had been acting up my last month of training was now sending regular stabs of pain down my back as the forty-pound backpack began to take its toll.

I felt emotional as the city of Escalante came into view, but surprisingly, the closer we got to the van the more numb I began to feel. My eleven-month journey to this place was concluding, but I was not feeling the big culmination of emotions I had expected.

We reached the van and offloaded our backpacks. There was a little confusion surrounding our rendezvous with Kathy, who had been staying at a local hotel and had hiked up the trail to meet us. Somehow, we had missed each other on the trail. While Patrick went off to search for her, the rest of us began to sort through our gear and load the trailer.

That completed, I was able to message with family and friends through my satellite communicator that I had completed my hike. As I sat in the van waiting for Kathy and Patrick to return, I received return texts from the kids. It was when I read them that I finally broke down. They expressed how proud they were of me for training and taking this trip. They admired me for finding a way to deal with my grief after losing their mother and the love of my life.

I had to walk away from the van as I was overwhelmed by emotion. I felt that through this journey I had somehow shown Claire, Morgan, and Carson that we can grieve and yet still move forward while holding Amy in our hearts forever. In that moment, I could feel Amy with me. I thought I heard her whisper, "Well done, Love."

Kathy and Patrick soon returned, and we headed into town for some well-deserved pizza and beer. I stared out the window on the drive back to Las Vegas, feeling more and more confident with every mile that this journey had been worth the toil, training, and emotional hardship I had endured. I know Amy would have been proud of me. As we neared Las Vegas, I kept rolling around in my head a line from one of my all-time favorite movies, *Shawshank Redemption*. Morgan had texted it to me just a few hours earlier: "Get busy living or get busy dying. That's goddamn right."

Amy is and will always be the love of my life. I know I still have a long way to go on this grief journey, but it's time to start planning my next adventure. I have some preliminary ideas under the go big or go home category, but I need to complete an honest self-assessment of my physical capabilities before I commit.

To everyone that reads this, I want to thank you for allowing me to share my journey with you. I will continue to write. It remains cathartic. It brings me joy and a degree of healing to share my memories and thoughts with others.

Please choose and spread joy every single day.

December 4, 2023 | Miles Hiked: 1,437

YES-MAN

I HAVE MADE IT THROUGH the first year of my grief journey. My trips to the Porkies, Pictured Rocks, and Grand Staircase-Escalante are in my rearview mirror, and I feel very good about all I have accomplished. Many have asked me if I plan to continue hiking. The answer is yes. I feel positive about the structured schedule and the benefits of physical exercise in my life. In addition to hiking, I curl in the cold weather months and have also picked up pickleball. You can find me on the court three or four times a week when the weather cooperates.

But I am still broken.

Morgan and I had a conversation the other night that struck me. He shared that he feels like a totally different person since his mother passed. I understood perfectly what he meant. There is an underlying sadness that permeates us. A gigantic void in our lives where Amy used to be. Life will never be the same for any of us. Her loss has no end. But we have to keep moving forward in the hope that by choosing joy every day we will honor her by living life to its fullest.

So, yes, I plan to continue to hike. This seems like a good time to announce that I will be taking two additional adventures in 2024.

Amy and I met in Colorado Springs at a work training. On our weekend off, a group of us decided to go whitewater rafting down the Arkansas River and the Royal Gorge. It was a fantastic memory for both of us. Most of the immediate family from the Youngquists, Pratts, and Gawrons will be joining me on a three-day, two-night whitewater rafting adventure down the Arkansas River and the Royal Gorge in memory of Amy. There are tentatively fourteen of us who will be able to make the trip. I know Amy would be delighted that we are going on this adventure and that so many of the family will be able to participate.

The trip is planned for early June 2024. While I am in Colorado, I also plan on taking a thirty-to-thirty-five-mile thru-hike of the Lost Creek Wilderness Area. I am not sure who, if any, of the family will join me for this portion of the trip, but I need to fold in some elevation into my training program.

I will need this training because I have planned something even bigger than my trip to Grand Staircase-Escalante. How big? Grand Canyon big! In late August, I will be joining a group from REI Adventures on a rim-to-rim hike of the Grand Canyon. After hiking the north Rim, we will descend nearly 6,000 feet down the North Kaibab Trail to Phantom Ranch. At the bottom of the

Grand Canyon, we will be afforded a free day to hike or simply relax around the ranch and cheer on the whitewater rafters down the Colorado River. The ascent out of the Grand Canyon will traverse the infamous Bright Angel Trail with an elevation gain of almost 5,000 feet.

Because permits for Phantom Ranch are limited, REI Adventures put me through a screening process, and I have been accepted for this journey. It will require even more training than this past year, and my goal will be to shed another twenty pounds before the trip. I am sure you will find me at a fitness center on an ascent trainer many days this winter and spring to mimic the elevation gains.

I would welcome anyone who wants to join me and share in this adventure. Some in my family have asked me why the Grand Canyon, and especially, why in late August? I took the latest trip available and know that it will be extremely hot down in the canyon. The average temp at the end of August is still over 100 degrees. REI Adventures has very experienced guides who go to great lengths to safeguard their hikers. This includes sometimes beginning the ascent in the middle of the night—1:00 a.m. I will be turning sixty on the Grand Canyon excursion and feel that I am not getting any younger. If I am going to do something big, at least big for me, I should do it while I am still in relatively good physical shape.

Seeing the Grand Canyon has always been on my bucket list. I always thought it would be something Amy and I would do together in our retirement. Now seems like the perfect time to tackle this challenge. The trip and the training will test me both physically and mentally.

Another goal of mine for 2024 does not involve crazy hikes in the heat of the summer. It involves being a better friend. Last year, I tried very hard to be a yes-man. I said yes to just about any invitation if I did not have scheduling conflicts, even when I did not feel up to it or when I knew that it would be a trigger for my grief. I think Amy and the kids are proud of me for that accomplishment.

Thank you to everyone that included me in your game nights, cooking endeavors, sporting events, vacations, lunches and dinners, golfing, weekend excursions, garden parties, campfires, pontoon rides, etc., etc.

This year I want to be a better friend and reach out to you all more. I will continue to be a yes-man, but don't be surprised to get invitations from me to do something out of the blue.

Choose and spread joy every day!

December 18, 2023 | Miles Hiked: 1,468

RESCUE HEROES

WHEN YOUR KIDS ARE growing up, it is natural for them to pretend to be heroes. Whether it is a fire fighter, police officer, soldier, doctor, or EMT, kids often spend hours pretending to be the heroes they see portrayed on television and in the movies.

When Morgan and Carson were very young, they tended to favor toys portraying these everyday heroes. Fortunately for us, Fisher Price offered the perfect toy for the boys, Rescue Heroes. With names like Billy Blazes, Wendy Waters, Jake Justice, Rocky Canyon, Ariel Flyer, and Jack Hammer, they offered kids the ability to engage in very positive imaginative play involving just about any vocation. Fisher Price even came out with cartoon videos for a short period of time.

As they grew older, Morgan and Carson showed a keen interest in their Uncle Chuck's career working for the Ramsey County Sheriff's Violent Crime Enforcement Team (VCET). During one visit to Milwaukee, their uncle took them sightseeing downtown to see the Harley Davidson Museum. He promised them lunch afterward—a sure way to win their heart.

My brother, not being familiar with the city, ended up taking them to an establishment in one of the rougher neighborhoods in Milwaukee. As they ate lunch, he casually pointed out the drug dealer in the parking lot. The boys were amazed that he could identify such an individual so easily.

He pointed out that the man was juggling multiple cell phones, seemed fidgety, had a decked-out automobile with heavily tinted windows, and was loitering in the parking lot of a fast-food restaurant. While they ate their lunch and continued to observe the individual, they witnessed at least two subtle drug transactions.

Amy and I were not really thrilled with this excursion, but it seemed to light a passion in the very impressionable Morgan and Carson. As they grew, our career choices offered them only computer screens, endless meetings, and frustrating corporate bureaucracies. It is no wonder that they both decided to pursue a career in law enforcement. At the University of Wisconsin-La Crosse, Morgan pursued a degree in Public Administration and Criminal Justice while Carson chose Sociology and Criminal Justice.

Both obtained meaningful internships during their college experience, one with the Madison Police Department and the other with the Division of Criminal Investigation, or DCI, the state of Wisconsin's version of the FBI.

Becoming a member of the law enforcement fraternity can be a long process. Both Morgan and Carson applied to the Madison Police Department in the fall of 2019. From applications, written tests and essays, to background checks, multiple interviews and psychiatric sessions, the process encompassed more than seven months. Both Morgan and Carson were accepted to the Madison Police Academy and began their training in late May 2020 during the pandemic.

Both were driven to excel and graduated in the top ten in their class at the academy. After finishing the academy, each graduate had to complete three months on the job with a training officer before they officially began their service.

Amy and I often were asked if we were "ok" with their career choice. We always chuckled when asked this question. As Amy would often and so eloquently state, "It is not my choice. I would have preferred something less risky, but they felt called to serve."

On Tuesday, March 23, 2021, at about 8:30 p.m., just a few weeks into their new careers, my phone rang. I did not recognize the number and almost let it go to voicemail, but the 608 area code for Madison caught my attention and made me pause. I decided I had better answer it just in case.

It was Morgan on the line. He had borrowed a cell phone from a fellow officer. He simply stated that he could not talk to me but wanted us to know he was safe and unharmed. Oh, and it probably would be best not to watch the news. The thirty-second phone call was understandably brief, but alarm bells were going off in my head. Amy and Claire were with me in the living room and immediately knew something had happened from the expression on my face.

Claire of course quickly got online to Madison news sources and learned that there had been an officer involved *critical incident*, meaning an officer had discharged their weapon. The only other detail we learned was that one individual was transported to University of Wisconsin Hospital with multiple gunshot wounds to the chest.

Our imaginations went wild with these tidbits as different scenarios played out in our heads. Rumors were circulating that a police officer had shot a suspect. As is often the case with initial reports, most of them strayed from the eventual truth.

Amy, Claire, and I immediately contacted our employers to notify them we would not be at work the next day so that we could go to Madison. We wanted to offer support for not only our boys but their colleagues and roommates on the force.

There are protocols for such incidents to preserve evidence and maintain the credibility of an officer's future testimony. We were not able to learn any of the details of the incident directly from Morgan until after his interviews and sworn statements were entered into the record. We eventually learned more accurate details from the media as they pieced together the story from eyewitness accounts and public information statements from the Madison Police Department.

Morgan and a fellow officer were outside a homeless shelter in Madison's North District. They were attempting to get an intoxicated individual admitted to detox. The homeless shelter would not take him due to his condition. While his fellow officer was on the phone in his squad car, Morgan was chatting with the individual when he heard several gunshots coming from inside the homeless shelter.

His reaction was pure training as he called into his radio, "Ed 2, shots fired!" and then ran into the building. As he entered, there was a throng of people running toward him, most keeping low to the floor. It was then he observed a man with a gun in one of the doorways leading to the communal sleeping area. As he ordered the man to drop his weapon, the individual went to raise his weapon. Morgan was able to get one shot off at the man before he ducked out of view behind the door.

Adrenaline was pumping as he raced into the next room. He found a man who had been shot several times. He survived, and a fellow resident and former medic in the armed forces was already administering first aid, allowing Morgan and his fellow officer to begin clearing the building.

They later learned from video that the suspect had fled out a back door immediately after being confronted. The man was apprehended four days later in Milwaukee and admitted to having a hit list of individuals at the shelter who had not treated him well. He had not anticipated the rapid police response.

Video from the homeless shelter's surveillance system showed that from the time the first shot was fired to when Morgan confronted the suspect, only four seconds elapsed.

A heavy police presence descended on the homeless shelter. This included Morgan's brother, Carson, who heard the call on the radio and raced to the scene.

Morgan was swept into critical incident protocols, including being patted down for injury, being isolated in an ambulance, and then being transported to a local hospital for drug testing. Shortly thereafter, he met with the union attorney on call for critical incidents. It is a sad state to realize that if a law enforcement officer discharges their weapon in the line of duty, it is standard procedure to treat them as a suspect until cleared.

The subsequent investigation was conducted by an independent law enforcement agency, in this case, Wisconsin's DCI. Their report was then reviewed by the district attorney, who determined Morgan's actions were justified. After this was complete, the Madison Police Department conducted an internal investigation to determine if Morgan had violated any policies and procedures. He was eventually cleared.

In the end, Morgan was on paid administrative leave for a period of four months before he was allowed to return to full duty.

On May 4, 2022, more than a year after the incident, Morgan was awarded the Medal of Valor for his rapid response and bravery in confronting an active shooter. Despite her chemotherapy schedule, Amy insisted we attend and celebrate this event.

There is a picture of our family together just after this ceremony. In the picture, Amy has the brightest smile with her head held high. She is literally beaming with pride at not only Morgan, but Carson and Claire standing beside her. She has her hand over her heart as if it were going to burst.

We never would have imagined this life path for either of our boys, but we are glad that they and their law enforcement brethren are out there keeping us safe every day. Heroes, all of them.

January 1, 2024 | Miles Hiked: 1,531

OGALLALA

JUST AFTER LABOR DAY 2023, one of Amy's lifelong friends, Laura, and her husband, Craig, invited me to their home, where they were hosting their second annual backyard concert. The performer was Trapper Schoepp, a local musician well-known on the Milwaukee and national music scene. Laura and Craig were lucky enough to have Trapper living on their block and willing to perform for the neighbors each year. I was happy to accept their invitation and jokingly told all my friends I was going to my first garden party!

I brought beverages and a comfortable camp chair and arrived twenty minutes before the show. Laura and Craig were excited to see me and went out of their way to make me feel welcome by introducing me to many of their neighbors. Their backyard was beautiful and just what I had envisioned for a garden party with flowers and blooming shrubs. Trapper was setting up on the deck with a colleague who was tuning an upright bass to accompany him.

He played a variety of covers including a Bob Dylan song and many originals of his own. One song caught my attention, "Ogallala." For those of you not familiar with this bustling metropolis of less than five thousand people in Western Nebraska, its claim to fame is that it is pretty much the only town in the western part of the state with a hotel and hospital of its own.

As Trapper was singing about being stranded for two nights in Ogallala during a blizzard, I leaned over and whispered to Laura that Amy and I also had a good tale about our stay in this town. She whispered back that she couldn't wait to read about it someday. I definitely don't want to disappoint her, so here is our Ogallala adventure.

In the summer of 2009, our family decided to take a vacation to Rocky Mountain National Park in Colorado. It was an awesome trip that included camping in our pop-up camper, hiking, whitewater rafting, horseback riding, and the traditional trips to the souvenir shop for locally made fudge and ice cream.

On our last day, we decided to hike to a mountain lake in the park before getting in the car and heading home. After a brief encounter with the local John Denver look alike, we headed up the trail with our waters and the boys' diabetes kit. The hike was popular with many hikers and climbers who made the moderately difficult trek up to a very picturesque lake sandwiched between two mountain peaks. We enjoyed lunch on the lakeshore and then headed back down the trail.

About halfway back to the trailhead, Morgan complained that he had to go to the bathroom. This was typically a sign that his blood sugar was too high. We took a quick break to check his levels, which were indeed high, and administered some additional insulin. He stubbornly refused to relieve himself along the path with so many people on the trail and insisted he could make it back to the trailhead.

The farther we hiked, however, the greater his urgency. Our pace increased from leisurely walk, to power walking, and then to a slight jog. Amy ran ahead with him, but he still refused to walk a few feet off trail to take care of business. Amy stumbled over a protruding root and nosedived hard onto the rocky path. Her knee was torn up pretty bad. We tried applying pressure to the wound, but it would not stop bleeding.

Fortunately, a passing rock climber stopped with a medical kit and kindly took the time to clean and sterilize the wound. He stated it was up to us, but he thought it was worth a trip to the emergency room for stitches. Amy managed to walk the remaining distance back to the parking lot at a slow pace where Morgan was finally able to visit the facilities.

We packed up and headed to the nearest ER. The ER doctor concurred with the rock climber that Amy's injury would need stitches. Claire had always been interested in the health care field, so in one of my less astute parenting moments, I suggested maybe she should observe them stitching Amy up. I am not sure what her true thoughts were, but she agreed to go in with her mother and watch the procedure. Amy admitted it was nice to have her there to distract her. Claire turned white as they cleaned the wound and stitched up Amy's knee. Claire and Amy held hands for most of the procedure until Claire had to make a quick exit before she passed out.

Meanwhile, I was getting anxious about our travel schedule. We had originally planned on trying to make it to Lincoln, Nebraska, on our return trip home, but our detour to the ER was setting back our timetable. By the time we left the ER, we were already three to four hours behind our goal.

After a brief stop to pick up some extra strength Tylenol, we hit the road. We were able to make Fort Collins, Colorado, around dinner time and stopped at the local McDonald's to let a severe storm pass before resuming our drive. On the road again, we set a good pace toward home but knew we were not going to make it as far as we wanted. Amy began looking at the map for a place to stop another two hundred miles down the road. Ogallala, Nebraska, leaped off the page as the only town likely to have a hotel for us to crash for the night.

We made Ogallala by around 9:00 p.m. and checked into a hotel. Our family returned to the car to grab overnight essentials and head to our room for the night. After grabbing everything we would need, I asked, "Who has the diabetes kit?"

My question was met with blank stares.

Amy and I immediately began tearing the car apart looking for it. The boys would need insulin before they went to bed. We keep backup insulin separately but had already transferred that to their kit because we had been running low. I must admit that I am typically the irrational individual when faced with a crisis, but in this case I remained calm.

For Amy, however, a dam of emotion burst forth. Whether she was just tired from the trip or from her visit to the ER, she uncharacteristically lost control of her emotions. We quickly deduced that we had left the kit in the McDonald's in Fort Collins. Round trip, that would be six or seven hours in the car to retrieve it. She demanded I give her the keys to the car so she could drive back to Fort Collins. We went back and forth on the wisdom of that course of action for about ten minutes.

Finally, cooler heads prevailed. I convinced her to take Morgan and Claire up to the room and call the McDonald's to confirm the diabetes kit had been found. Meanwhile, I would take Carson to the local hospital and see if I could procure enough insulin to make it back home.

It was our second trip to an emergency room that day. The ER doctor met with us and patiently listened to our story. Unfortunately, the ER did not have access to insulin, and the pharmacies in town had closed hours earlier. He did indicate, however, that the diabetes clinic likely had some sample insulin pens. But the clinic was locked up. After some discussion with his colleagues, it was decided that they would break into the clinic and retrieve them for us. It was with great relief and gratitude that we came away from the ER with two sample insulin pens with enough insulin to get us home the next day.

When Carson and I returned to the hotel, we found a calmer Amy. Claire had remembered that the McDonald's we had visited was next to a Sam's Club, and they were able to identify the correct restaurant and call them. They had the diabetes kit and would ship it to us the next day. Carson and I shared our successful visit to the ER, and everyone let out a big sigh of relief. Our stay in Ogallala would never be forgotten.

As Trapper played and the night progressed, I thought of how much Amy would have enjoyed coming to this event. She loved live performances, and the intimate setting was special. Trapper did not play dance music, but Amy would have found a way. I'm sure of that. I am very grateful that Laura and Craig were kind enough to include me. I can't wait to go next year!

January 15, 2024 | Miles Hiked: 1,555

RUINED

TODAY MY GRIEF HAS been triggered. I thought I was doing well after weathering the first-year mark, only to be derailed by the holidays and Amy's upcoming birthday. Unboxing the Christmas decorations for the house and decorating our joy tree gave me a push into melancholy.

Last night, I had a late draw at curling and got back after midnight. I thought it best to skip my sleep medication so I wouldn't be too groggy in the morning. All I succeeded in doing was fostering dreams of Amy throughout the night. I woke up several times in tears with only Macc and Beau to console me.

My dreams were crazy and incoherent, but one of them brought back a very painful memory. As Amy's cancer progressed, one afternoon she broke down into tears and became distraught. When I came into the room, I asked her what was going on. She sobbed, "I've *ruined* everyone's lives!"

I was at a loss for words as I hugged and held her. Finally, I told her to look at me. Our eyes locked, and I said in my firmest tone, "Sweetie, you have done nothing but *enriched* our lives. Don't *ever* doubt that." This seemed to calm her. We managed to pass the afternoon talking about the kids before a baseball game came on, and she was able to doze off.

As I recalled this memory, I was on the verge of tears. I reached out to my friend Joe and let him know I was having a rough day. I asked him if he had lunch plans. He did, but in typical Joe fashion, he said he would be at my place by 3:30 p.m. or so and we could grab dinner together. I tried to keep busy most of the day running errands, but I continued to struggle as the day progressed. My tears ebbed and flowed every time a certain song played from my playlist or I glanced at the many pictures of Amy displayed throughout the house.

I cooked my famous golosh for dinner and sat down at my computer to finish some Christmas shopping while I waited for Joe to arrive.

His visit was good for me to distract myself from my own thoughts. I learned more of his plans to start his own coaching consulting practice in 2024. It was nice to think about something else for a time, but Joe eventually and deftly steered the conversation back to my real reason for calling. I unloaded my feelings on him, and it felt good to share the successes and setbacks of my grief journey.

Joe is a brother to me. His visit only lasted a couple of hours, but I felt infinitely better afterward. I felt more centered on the joy Amy brought to our lives. The moral of the story? Never hesitate to phone a friend. Thanks, brother.

January 29, 2024 | Miles Hiked: 1,569

A FOWL ODOR

IN EARLY NOVEMBER, I returned from visiting my cousin and his wife near Myrtle Beach, South Carolina. I stopped at New River Gorge National Park in West Virginia on my way out and got in twelve miles of hiking to break up the long drive. I was able to play some golf and introduce my cousin Tom to pickleball. It was my first time back to the area since our family vacation/baseball tournament there in 2010.

Morgan and Carson played for the Sussex Hawks during their U-12 baseball season. It was the year the program typically sent their teams to the Baseball Hall of Fame in Cooperstown, New York, to participate in a tournament. The format of the tournament included the players being boarded on-site at the baseball complex for the entirety of the tournament away from their families.

Because of their diabetes, Amy and I did not feel comfortable with the arrangement. Fortunately, the team was open to an alternative destination where we could better monitor and manage their diabetes. Thus, we ended up traveling to Ripken Baseball for a tournament in Myrtle Beach. I don't believe the other parents were too disappointed to be headed to a beach destination instead of upstate New York.

We had an awesome trip and enjoyed time poolside with their teammates and beach time as a family. Amy loved the ocean, and my memories of her with the kids in the water and sand will be etched in my memory forever. The weather was so fantastic that we decided to stay an extra day and long haul it home in one day instead of two.

We began our journey home at 6:00 a.m. After a delay in Tennessee due to AC problems, we continued our long drive home. By the time we reached Chicago, my fingers and hands began to cramp from gripping the steering wheel for so long. We powered through and pulled into our driveway at 1:00 a.m. We were all drained and wanted to crash in our beds and unpack the next morning.

When we opened the garage door, we were greeted by a foul odor. We quickly surmised that the refrigerator in our garage had bit the dust while we were on vacation. This had given the various meats contained in the freezer ample time to become a toxic cocktail of rancid juice and spoiled meat, creating a noxious puddle at the base of the refrigerator. Foremost among the meat was a fifteen-pound turkey that looked and felt more like a giant marshmallow than a delicious meal.

Amy wanted to dive in and begin cleaning this mess immediately, but I just couldn't do it. The kids and I were exhausted from the long drive home and wanted nothing more than to go to sleep. Amy and I exchanged a few stern words about our priorities, and I won the argument by simply stating she could do what she wanted, but I was going to bed. She reluctantly agreed to wait until morning.

Amy was obsessive compulsive about cleaning. I know she couldn't sleep much with this task waiting for us in the morning. While I slept, she developed a strategy. We would empty the meat in the refrigerator into a plastic bin. Because garbage day was still several days away, she thought we could dispose of the meat at the dumpster at the Village Park. We would then empty and recycle all of the bottles and cans that had been contaminated by the rancid meat juice. The last task would be sterilizing the refrigerator with bleach and placing it all curbside for pickup on garbage day.

At 6:00 a.m., Amy woke me. She was intent on getting an early start to executing her plan. When she shared it with me, I grudgingly agreed, figuring it would be better to dispose of the meat with less people up and about. I did make one change to her plan, however. I insisted that the plastic bin of foul meat would not enter either of our cars even with the windows down!

Amy donned yellow rubber cleaning gloves and with a bandana over her mouth she emptied the meat into the plastic bin. I busted out the bungee cords and strapped the meat filled plastic bin to the top of our Ford Expedition. We drove slowly to a remote corner of Village Park. I can only imagine how any neighbors who saw us interpreted this strange site. We dumped the container into the dumpster and made a quick getaway.

Later that morning, we confessed our deed to a neighbor. They kindly called the Village claiming they had been running past the dumpster and reported the smell emanating from it. They were reassured that a garbage truck would be dispatched to empty the dumpster.

The refrigerator turned out to be a tougher job. No matter how many times Amy and I scrubbed the inside of the beast with bleach, we could not rid it of its rancid smell. We removed the doors and put it out by the curb to be picked up by the disposal company on garbage day.

Hundreds of flies immediately found it and feasted on whatever microscopic morsels remained for them. As people passed the refrigerator while walking their dogs, our family got twisted pleasure watching the dogs go crazy to get to the refrigerator and then seeing its smell hit their owners. Faces contorted in the most amusing ways as the odor hit their nose. Most would immediately cross to the other side of the street.

We were grateful when garbage day arrived, knowing the refrigerator would be hauled off. To my surprise, the local junk guy, a regular who cruised through the neighborhood looking for salvageable furniture and other items before the garbage trucks arrived, stopped when he saw the refrigerator. I was mortified as he loaded the fetid thing into the back of his minivan. I cannot imagine the stench he put up with on his drive home, but I was relieved to finally rid it from my front yard.

I am grateful to my cousin Tom and his wife Kathy for their hospitality during my visit. This time, my grief was not triggered by the flood of memories brought on by my return to Myrtle Beach. Instead, I recall the fowl incident with fondness. I can't help but smile and chuckle when I envision Amy in her rubber gloves and bandana that morning. A small victory.

February 12, 2024 | Miles Hiked: 1,605

KEY LIME PIE

FROM VERY EARLY IN her diagnosis, my goal was to make every day the best day it could possibly be for Amy. Thus began our new approach to life. We jokingly referred to this new philosophy as the Year of No Budget. We would not hold back from anything we wanted to do out of financial concerns. We would forge ahead with whatever made Amy happy or could distract her from her treatments.

The first purchase under this philosophy was a new bed with an adjustable base. The metastasized cancer in her chest paralyzed her left vocal cord. Whether it was from the acid reflux or the difficulty breathing, Amy could only sleep sitting upright. She could not lay flat. We had improvised with a reading pillow, but we needed a more permanent solution, and the adjustable frame solved this problem perfectly.

Being able to travel with this limitation posed a challenge for us. Fortunately, my brother-in-law Jerry designed and built a portable device that would adjust any mattress to five or six upright positions. We affectionately called it *the contraption*. It worked perfectly and gave Amy the assurance that she would be comfortable whenever we traveled.

We laid plans to take a chemo vacation to Florida at the end of February assuming her cancer markers continued to trend in the right direction. We let our dear friend Jackie plan an adventure for us. In addition to our traditional sanctuary to their condo, we would venture down into the Keys with stops in Islamorada and Key West.

Amy was apprehensive about flying, so we procured gummies of a medicated nature that she took on her way to the airport. It worked to perfection, and she slept comfortably most of the flight and car ride from Tampa to Siesta Key.

We arrived to beautiful weather and took the first couple of days to transition to vacation mode. We spent time at numerous establishments enjoying the water views and libations. Without a doubt though, Amy's favorite part of the day was our nightly conversations with Joe and Jackie on their lanai. No subject was off limits, and we often had silly and wild conversations that got us all laughing. Something we needed desperately. We made sure that Amy got plenty of rest though, even if we had to cut her lanai time short each night.

After a few days, we headed south toward Highway 1 and the Keys. Jackie found the most wonderful accommodations for us in both locations that made it easier for Amy to relax and just enjoy the sunshine and warm temperatures. Our first night was in Islamorada. The Vrbo was at Little Basin Villas and included a heated pool just off the dock and offered plentiful sunshine.

We ran into a problem on our first night, however. It was a pleasant evening, and we thought we would walk to a local establishment just a couple of blocks down the road. Joe and Jackie went ahead to scout out a table on the beach. Amy struggled. Within the first hundred yards, she was exhausted from her chemo treatment a few days earlier. She was in tears as we slowly made our way to the restaurant. I knew then that we would not be able to do the simple tasks we had once taken for granted.

Later, when I was alone with Joe, I let him know Amy and I needed to Uber everywhere, even if it was across the street. Joe and Jackie immediately picked up on our needs and volunteered to get a head start to the restaurants and establishments the rest of the trip, allowing Amy to rest longer and avoid strenuous exercise.

We set aside time in the afternoons for Amy to nap and rest. One afternoon, she curled up on the couch of our Vrbo and fell asleep under her courage blanket given to her by one of her high school friends. As I watched her sleep, I contemplated our future, and my thoughts turned dark. She began to stir after a couple of hours, and I vowed not to let my thoughts intrude on this trip.

We moved south to Key West and found a better rhythm. On the first night, we took in Key West's infamous sunset. Amy and I danced as the sun set behind us. I will admit, not all of my thoughts were of the moment, but were instead contemplating how many more moments with Amy I might be afforded.

Jackie had found us a hotel on the water in Key West that boasted its own beach and private pool area. Amy and I did not stray from the hotel except for nightly meals and a bar or two. Each night, we returned to the hotel while Jackie and Joe continued to explore Key West.

After I got her settled into bed with *the contraption* propping up her mattress, Amy sent me out in search of a piece of Key lime pie. The doctor had assured us that no calories were bad calories when you are on chemo. The first couple of nights I was able to obtain them at the pool bar.

One night, we had a late dinner at a very nice restaurant on the other side of the island. We were seated next to legendary football coach Dick Vermeil. By the time we returned to our room for the night, the kitchen was closed.

I felt panic. With everything Amy was going through, there was no way I was coming back to the room without her Key lime pie. I begged the pool bartender to sneak into the kitchen and smuggle out a piece for me. He finally agreed to try after he served another couple waiting for their drinks. I nervously waited for him to return and was relieved to see him walk back in with a to-go bag. I tipped him generously and returned to our room with my prize.

Amy was curious why I was away so long, but I deflected her by telling her there was a large party in the pool area and I had to wait to get service. I did not want her to know how desperate I had become to procure her pie. As usual, she only ate half, leaving me the remainder.

As she dozed off to sleep that night, I contemplated our trip to Key West. I was saddened. I had hoped the trip would be filled with small moments of happiness and memories. Maybe I just can't see it now, but mostly, I feel pain and guilt at furthering Amy's struggles by taking her away from where she was most comfortable.

Perhaps my feelings will fade with time. But I doubt I will ever be able to return to Key West . . . or enjoy a piece of Key lime pie.

February 26, 2024 | Miles Hiked: 1,657

MO-MO TWINS

PARENTS LOOK FORWARD TO the birth of their children with anticipation and joy. There is a reason *What to Expect When You're Expecting*, written by Heidi Murkoff, continues to be one of Amazon's best sellers. This book is a must read for all first-time parents.

Amy and I were no different. We read this book when we were expecting Claire, and we reread it when we decided to have a second child. Sometimes though, not everything goes according to plan.

After getting a positive result on a home pregnancy test, Amy and I were excited for her ob-gyn appointment, where they would take the first ultrasound. They ushered us into the exam room and a nurse shortly came in to conduct the procedure. She applied the gel and began looking for the baby. She found it and gave us a quick glance of him on the monitor as we listened to his heartbeat. As she began taking measurements, she suddenly said, "Oh, it looks like there are two in here."

Amy and I stared at each other in disbelief. Then, both our faces lit up with wide grins as we began to laugh at the curveball life had just thrown at us. The nurse continued to take measurements as we began to contemplate what this would mean for the pregnancy and our lives.

At some point, we noticed that the nurse was no longer smiling but had become focused on the ultrasound. She completed her tasks and indicated the doctor would be in shortly. After a few minutes, the doctor came in and congratulated us on expecting twins. She talked to Amy at length about how this pregnancy would be different than Amy's first. After reviewing that, she mentioned that the ultrasound had failed to detect a membrane that would normally separate the twins.

Our mood turned serious in an instant.

"What does that mean?" we asked.

She explained that normally the babies are each contained in their own amniotic sac. An ultrasound would typically show the membrane of these two sacs that separate the babies. The doctor quickly added that this membrane is sometimes difficult to see early in the pregnancy and that we should not be alarmed that they could not find it. She said that we would do another ultrasound on our next visit, and there was nothing that we should do differently.

Reassured, we headed home to share our exciting news with family, friends, and neighbors. My mother was a twin, and I couldn't wait to share the news with her. When we got her on the line and shared the news, we received a very subdued congratulations. Shortly thereafter, she asked if I had spoken to my sister lately. After hanging up, both Amy and I were bewildered at my mother's subdued reaction.

It made total sense, though, after we called to share the news with my sister. Evidently, just prior to our call, my sister had also called Mom to tell her that she was expecting. My mom was in a total state of shock after getting the news that she would have three new grandchildren sometime in January!

Our life progressed normally for the next several weeks as Amy had bouts of nausea. Like the first pregnancy, she slept quite a bit, which left lots of quality time for me with Claire. We arrived optimistic at the next ob-gyn appointment.

The nurse began the ultrasound, and we became quiet as she found the twins and took measurements to chart their growth. As the procedure dragged on, both Amy and I were thinking the same thing—she's not finding it.

Worry began to creep in the longer the procedure dragged on. Finally, she completed the ultrasound and told us the doctor would be in soon. Amy gripped my hand tight as we waited in silence. The doctor eventually came in and shared the news we suspected. The ultrasound had not revealed a membrane. The doctor indicated that she wanted to look herself, so we started the procedure over again.

As she looked for the membrane, she turned the monitor toward us so we could also see as she pointed out each twin to us. After a good ten minutes, she also could not find any separating membrane. She explained that in rare cases where the egg splits late after the placenta has already formed, twins will sometimes, but very rarely, share the same amniotic sac. Those cases are referred to as monoamniotic twins, or Mo-Mo twins, and are only 1 percent of all twin pregnancies. Our doctor had never seen Mo-Mo twins in her practice until now. She did not hold back as she explained that this would be a high-risk pregnancy. The main danger would be cord entanglement as the babies grew larger in the later stages of the pregnancy.

She explained that sometimes the membrane can be very, very thin and not show up on a standard ultrasound when twins split late. Her plan for us would be to proceed normally. There was really no procedure or drug available that could help the situation. She recommended we see a perinatologist, a maternal–fetal medicine specialist in high-risk pregnancies, once Amy's pregnancy reached twenty-four weeks. At that time, they could do a color flow doppler high resolution ultrasound to see how the twins were progressing and to look for the membrane again.

Our takeaway from the appointment was that there was nothing we nor the medical professionals could do in the immediate future. Amy latched onto that and was determined to control what she could. She would take especially good care of herself, eat healthy, exercise, and most of all, not let herself get mentally stressed by the situation.

Unfortunately, I often take the opposite approach. I want to learn everything I possibly can about the situation I am facing so that I can make the best decisions possible. I delved into learning everything I could about monoamniotic twins. In 1997, there was precious little information about the subject online and only two paragraphs devoted to the condition in a text I found at the Medical College of Wisconsin.

Most of the information I gathered was from other parents of expecting Mo-Mo twins. Their doctors, however, had varying approaches to their pregnancies. Before long, I became a central hub of email correspondence between parents seeking information just like me. Together with another parent, we started a chat room to document all the posts, discussions, and outcomes. At the time, we did not envision the chat room would become a central hub of information for parents for over twenty years.

The scariest bit of information I learned was that the mortality rate for Mo-Mo twins was extremely high, between 40 and 60 percent.

Amy was understanding of my attempts to learn more, but she stated very firmly that I was not to share any information with her. She wanted to stay focused on her health and on remaining positive. Despite her bravado, I know she was very worried, but I concluded that stress could only have a negative effect on her and the babies' well-being, so as she requested, I kept the information I learned to myself.

Amy shined during the next couple of months. She remained upbeat and excited for the arrival of the twins. We moved Claire to a new bedroom and prepared the twins' new room. We were able to obtain another crib from our friends who had twins previously, saving us some money.

Everything was going very smoothly as the time for our appointment with the perinatologist neared. The first week in October, Amy's mother, Judy, came over to babysit Claire as we headed off to our big appointment. They ushered us into a specialized exam room with the color flow doppler machine. We both were nervous as the doctor came in and, after a short introduction, began the procedure. Amy and I attempted to chat with him to relieve some of our nervous tension, but the doctor politely asked us to remain quiet while he concentrated on the procedure.

It seemed like forever as he leaned in towards his monitor looking for the membrane. Amy squeezed my hand tight as the moments dragged on. Five minutes, then ten minutes, then fifteen minutes. Both Amy and I began to tense up. Finally, the doctor let out a huge sigh and sat back in his chair and stated simply, "I found it."

Our faces lit up as he showed us the very thin membrane. He said we should return to our normal ob-gyn and that it looked like the twins were doing extremely well with no twin-to-twin transfusion syndrome (TTTS), where blood flows unequally between the twins.

Amy and I were all smiles as we walked to the car on that late afternoon in October. The sun was creeping toward the horizon as we got into the car. We took a moment to hug and release the emotions and stress of the past couple of months. We cried together for several minutes and then began to laugh before heading home to share the fantastic news with our families.

I've always admired Amy's positivity, but never more so than those awful weeks of uncertainty and worry in 1997.

March 11, 2024 | Miles Hiked: 1,695

TWO MOCKINGBIRDS

EVERY MONTH I HAVE lunch with my friend Jared. I met Jared through my employer and worked with him for many years before our lives became irrevocably linked. Jared's wife, Lana, was diagnosed with colon cancer approximately one year before Amy's diagnosis. I would occasionally bump into Jared at the UW Cancer Center at ProHealth Care amid our wives' tests and chemotherapy.

Lana and Amy passed within two weeks of each other in the fall of 2022.

Like Amy, Lana celebrated and embraced life. She was a delight whenever our paths crossed at a local restaurant or shop. Jared, Lana, and their two daughters, Maddie and Isabel, encourage everyone to Live Like Lana, much like our family seeks to inspire everyone to Choose Joy every day.

During our October lunch, he mentioned that he had purchased season tickets to the Marcus Performing Arts season including a production of Harper Lee's *To Kill a Mockingbird*, featuring Richard Thomas as Atticus Finch. I was hit by a tsunami of memories and emotions because this book had special significance for Amy and me.

Early in our relationship, Amy and I would often pass time together reading to each other. One of the very first books we read together was *To Kill a Mockingbird*. The timeless story of Scout, Jem, Dill, Jim, Bo, and Atticus resonated with us. We both thought it was a masterpiece highlighting the loss of innocence in many different ways through humor and storytelling. The phrase "to kill a mockingbird" is actually only mentioned once in the book. The mockingbird represents innocence, as its only function is to sing sweet melodies for everyone to enjoy. To kill one—an innocent—is a sin.

The book continued to influence our lives. Claire's middle name is Louise, a nod to Jean Louise, the main character of the novel. Her nickname, Scout, also became beloved in our family after we named our second English springer spaniel Scout.

As a stay-at-home mom for the early infant and toddler years, Amy's life was filled with diapers, meals, playtime, and interaction with other neighborhood kids. She *loved* being a mother. But it was an exhausting and demanding role. One year, I bought season tickets to the Marcus Performing Arts Center for us. I theorized that having the tickets in hand would force us to get a babysitter at least once each month to have a date night away from the kids.

Our first outing we had dinner at Benihana in downtown

Milwaukee before taking in the performance. The show was *Anything Goes*, a musical featuring the music and lyrics of Cole Porter. Despite the musical numbers, Amy was asleep on my shoulder by the middle of the first act.

Our neighboring seatmates turned and gave me annoyed looks as Amy began to gently snore. I didn't mind. I just gave a small shrug and smiled. She deserved every minute of extra sleep she could get. We left during intermission and grabbed a custard treat before going home and resuming our parental roles. After that episode, we changed our tickets to matinee shows followed by dinner to avoid the post meal siesta.

Another strategy employed by Amy to get more adult interaction involved our good friend Peg. Amy and Peg, inspired by Oprah's Book of the Month Club, started their own book club. The first gathering was on April 15, 1999, where a small group of women read *Where the Heart Is* by Billie Letts.

My first experience with the group was at their second meeting the following month when Amy hosted. The book was *A Separate Peace* by John Knowles. At some point in their discussion and after a few glasses of wine, they were interrupted by noises in the front yard. The group en masse exited the house to investigate. A few wild turkeys had wandered into our front lawn and were strutting around. When the excitement abated and the group returned to their discussion, it was decided the book club would be named the Wild Turkeys Book Club.

Amy enjoyed her time with this strong group of women. As the years progressed, they added an annual retreat to the agenda that included destinations from Charleston, South Carolina, to Door County, Wisconsin. There are approximately fifteen members of the current group, and a new generation is being welcomed with Claire, Hayley, and other daughters now beginning to participate.

Of course, *To Kill a Mockingbird* made the list of books read by this group in 2008. I could not pass up an opportunity to see the stage adaptation with Jared. I purchased a ticket, and Jared and I shared a meal prior to the production.

I was elated at their adaptation. Unlike the movie released in 1962 starring Gregory Peck, the stage adaptation retained much of the humor of the book intertwined within the serious underpinnings of the story.

As I reflect on the book and the play, I realize that Lana and Amy's lives were like the mockingbird's song, a beautiful melody of love and joy that enriched the lives of family, friends, and even total strangers.

The loss of that song leaves a void in the world. But I hear the notes of a new melody, still faint, but growing louder each day. Claire, Morgan, Carson, Maddie, and Isabel will one day make it a symphony. Amy and Lana. Two mockingbirds. What a magnificent legacy.

March 25, 2024 | Miles Hiked: 1,727

PATTERNS

SEVERAL YEARS AGO, AMY and I went out to dinner with our friends Joe and Jackie to Tenuta's Italian Restaurant in the Bayview neighborhood of Milwaukee. We loved small intimate restaurants like this, and Tenuta's did not disappoint. The food was exceptional, and the atmosphere is special.

As is often the case with Joe and Jackie, the conversation ranged from serious to absurd. At some point in the evening, the subject wandered to what individual we would each reserve as our one-off impossible one-night stand. It was a funny discussion, and we each tried to guess the other's one-off. Of course, I already knew Amy's was a younger Michael McDonald, and I gave her my blessing for this one-night tryst if the opportunity ever materialized.

Aided by the wine and cocktails, the conversation continued along this silly thread. It morphed into what would happen if each of us were to lose our spouse. I stated that I doubted whether I would ever remarry. When asked for a rationale, I simply stated—aided by one too many Captain and Cokes—that I had won the (expletive) lottery when I met Amy, and I could never expect to be so lucky ever again.

Amy got quiet and softly told me to stop teasing her.

I gently replied, "I'm not teasing you. I mean every word. I won the lottery when you came into my life."

She squeezed my hand, and the conversation moved on to other subjects as we enjoyed our evening.

I have discovered that the community of surviving spouses is surprisingly large. From young to old, I have met men and women who have walked this incredibly difficult and sad journey. I have believed from the beginning that everyone's journey is different. There are no right or wrong approaches for how to deal with the loss of a spouse.

For example, it was painful for me to have Amy's clothes in the closet. I woke up every morning to the crushing reminder that Amy was no longer with us. On the other hand, I have a friend who finds great comfort in seeing their spouse's clothing every morning.

One of the biggest shocks to my system, however, came when a widowed friend shared with me their intention to take off their wedding ring. This upset me. I don't know why it bothered me, but maybe it was because I could not imagine taking my wedding ring off. I also continue to wear Amy's wedding ring on a necklace around my neck every day.

I turned to the omniscient portal of all knowledge, the internet, for an answer. As I anticipated, I found only opinions with no definitive standard. Over the next few weeks, I realized that this is a deeply personal decision and that there are no right or wrong answers to this question. Some have taken their wedding ring off shortly after their spouse's passing, and others continue to wear it years afterward. I have not observed a correlation to where grieving spouses are in their grief journeys and concluded I should not judge anyone for their decision.

This week I had dinner with my friend Jim. I asked him to share any observations he may have regarding my journey. He shared with me that overall he thought I was making steady progress. There are no timetables for grief, but he thought my writing and hiking had very positive impacts on my journey.

He also gently guided me about breaking patterns. For example, last fall I organized a dinner out for him and his fiancée, Michelle, and another couple. I made a reservation at the same restaurant that we had gathered with Amy almost a year earlier. He knew this would be a difficult dinner for all of us. More so than if I had picked a different restaurant. He theorized I had selected the restaurant so as to include Amy or the memory of Amy in our gathering. I sat back in contemplation. He was correct. In retrospect, I could have made a healthier decision for myself and the others.

My rational self knows that Amy wants me to be happy and to not dwell in sadness and grief. I need to be open to new friendships and experiences. I need to strike out in new ways that make me feel uncomfortable. To break old patterns and forge a new path.

Hiking and writing have helped move me toward this new life and have been good for my mental health. But my friend's words were nudging me toward applying that same philosophy to other aspects of my life as well. To break patterns, routines, and habits that keep me static in my grief. I will be looking for those opportunities in the months ahead.

I am grateful for Jim's sage advice and hope to do better. But for now, taking off my wedding ring is simply a bridge too far.

April 8, 2024 | Miles Hiked: 1,742

THAT'S MY MAMA!

BASEBALL HAS ALWAYS BEEN the dominant sport in the Youngquist household. From the earliest of ages, Morgan and Carson were out in the yard playing catch. Claire played softball for a few years, but she was more a student of the game. She watched baseball with Amy and me and was astute enough to grasp its strategic underpinnings and pastoral elegance.

One of our first dates as a couple was to a Milwaukee Brewers game. We tailgated outside old County Stadium, played cribbage, and enjoyed the sunshine. I always teased Amy that she did not remember who was playing (Seattle), but she did remember that the Brewers came out on top that day.

After several years in Milwaukee, I was invited to join the Cream City Fantasy Baseball League, a group of eight gentlemen who also loved the game. This group formed long before fantasy sports took off with the advent of online stats and drafts. The two founders created the league with the goal of making it as realistic and true to the game as possible. Thus, there is no draft, but each team is afforded a $260 budget, and the season begins with an auction of available players. The general managers have to stay within their $260 salary cap and balance their rosters with offensive stats that earn them runs and pitching stats that earn them subtraction of runs against their opponents.

In the early years of the league, before the advent of email, each general manager had to submit their weekly rosters by mail. It was controversial when one year a general manager showed up with a laptop computer! Now it is the norm for everyone to have a computer or tablet to organize their auction strategies using the latest news feeds and online rankings.

My team, the Sussex Sharks, managed by Niccolo Machiavelli, has notoriously never won the championship. One year I hosted the auction. When Claire came home, she reviewed my player acquisitions and proceeded to critique me in front of my fellow general managers. I have never lived that moment down and continue to get jibes from them yearly about Claire's thoughts on my strategies.

Another year, Amy came home during the auction. On the counter was the coveted Cream City traveling trophy. It was designed to be as big and tacky as possible. When Amy noticed the trophy, she went out of her way to fawn over it, and told the group, "So this is what the championship trophy looks like. Thank goodness it won't ever be displayed in our house!" Another comment that continues to be brought up every year at our annual auction.

When Morgan and Carson were little, they loved baseball so much that I had to lie about their age to get them into their first baseball league. They only accepted players who were five years old or older. They wanted to play on a team so bad that I lied about their age and signed them up as four-year-olds. Obviously, I also had to volunteer to coach the team.

As the years went by, they developed into pretty good players and made several select teams. When they were in high school, they joined one of the three or four elite programs in Milwaukee at the time, STIKS Baseball Academy. Morgan was a left-handed pitcher and played first base. Carson was a catcher.

Unfortunately, the boys were plagued by injuries or freak accidents. Over their careers, both Morgan and Carson were frequent fliers at local hospitals and clinics. Morgan with a hip pointer and elbow issues and Carson with just plain freak accidents that seemed to always find him while on the field.

Our baseball travels took us far and wide from the Atlantic Ocean to the red clay of Georgia and the cornfields of Iowa. During their freshman season on STIKS, the team travelled to Georgia for a large Perfect Game Tournament. The team played well but fell short in bracket play. Their last game took place at a local high school. During the middle innings, Carson accomplished a feat I have never witnessed before and likely will never see again. He fouled a ball off his bat directly into his face. Because of his diabetes and a possible concussion, he was transported to Emory University Hospital in downtown Atlanta. Amy of course rode in the ambulance with him. Fortunately, it was only a broken nose.

When they were sophomores in high school, their team was entered into a Perfect Game Tournament in Iowa. Amy and I made the trek to Des Moines to watch the boys play. Their team did not do particularly well and ended up playing in a consolation game against another Milwaukee-based select team.

At some point in the game, one of the opposing players hit a high foul ball in front of the third base dugout. Carson and Cam, their team's third baseman, converged on the ball. The two collided at full speed with Carson's arm outstretched reaching for the ball. His arm hit Cam's chest, and both went down in a tangled mess.

That's when the screaming started. Carson writhed on the ground holding his arm. He had dislocated his elbow. It seemed like forever for the EMTs to arrive and immobilize his arm with an air cast before taking an ambulance ride to the local hospital. In the ER, an x-ray quickly confirmed the diagnosis. We had to wait for the orthopedic specialist on call to arrive at the hospital. While we were waiting, nature called, so a nurse and I helped Carson relieve himself into a bedpan.

The orthopedic doctor arrived after about a forty-five-minute wait. Carson was given some strong pain medication in anticipation of the doctor resetting the bones. He reviewed the x-ray and asked for the family to wait down the hall. Amy, Morgan, and I all winced as we heard Carson scream in agony when the doctor reset his elbow.

The nurse came and indicated we could rejoin Carson. I have heard stories of people losing their inhibitions while on pain medicine, and YouTube is flush with examples. Carson did not disappoint.

When Amy appeared in the doorway to Carson's room, he very loudly proclaimed to the entire emergency room, "Mama! That's my Mama!"

Amy smiled from ear-to-ear at the proclamation from her six-foot, four-inch, two-hundred-pound, fifteen-year-old son. It was said with such love and enthusiasm it made everyone smile.

When his *identical* twin brother—who was recording the entire incident—entered the room, Carson declared, "Morgan! You are soooooo handsome!"

Amy, Morgan, and I, as well as the nursing staff, were all laughing, but Carson was not done yet. When he saw me, he became serious and lowered his voice. "Dad! I remember."

"Remember what?" I asked.

"You helped me," he declared, referring to the bedpan.

I didn't want to embarrass him, so I quickly shrugged it off and simply said, "Yes, I did."

His response was an instant classic. "Impressive, wasn't it!"

The entire room burst out laughing. His brother had captured the moment on video, but I told Morgan directly, "You are never to post this to social media. He will never live it down."

Our families love of baseball comes not only from the game, but from the hours and hours we spent together as a family traveling all over the country, dinners and lunches with teammates, waiting for games to begin, and watching the boys play.

Given baseball was such an integral part of our family life, it was only fitting that we said goodbye to Amy at a baseball field. Her celebration of life was held at Wisconsin Brewing Company Park, home of the Lake Country DockHounds.

The visitation line started in the clubhouse and snaked down the stairs for hours. The funeral directors eventually asked the family to work down the line so that we could start with the memorial portion of the gathering.

Baseball will always be an integral part of our family, and we have countless hours of happy memories with Amy, whether it was on the side of the freeway watching the boys trying to stretch out cramps from an earlier game or watching Amy fall asleep to a game only to have her wake up with a start and ask us for the score.

There really are only two seasons in the Youngquist household: baseball season and the off-season.

April 22, 2024 | Miles Hiked: 1,807

ATLAS

WHEN CARSON WAS IN high school, he worked hard to earn a scholarship to play baseball in college. The spring of his junior year he received a verbal offer from a college for a scholarship. Although excited, we knew a verbal offer was not binding, so he continued to work hard.

When he touched base with the coach early in the summer between his junior and senior year, the coach rescinded his offer. He explained he had pressing positional needs and had to go in a different direction.

Carson was devastated. He went from playing Division 1 baseball to no offers at any level. To make matters worse, he dislocated his elbow playing in the spring and his recruiting season was lost. Carson sulked in his room for several days and moped through life after this setback. After about a week, I passed by his door and saw him once again lying in bed in a morose mood.

I paused in the doorway searching for the right words. I've never considered myself to have great parental wisdom or insight. That was Amy's forte. But in this case, Carson shared with me years later he never forgot what I told him.

"Son," I said, "sometimes life isn't fair. I know you deserved that offer, but it's gone. There is nothing you can do about it. I know it has been a blow to your goals. For the past week, I've given you space and let you deal with your feelings. But it is time to pick yourself up, leave your room, and get back to work."

He claims I added "before I kick you in the ass," but I don't recall using that phrase. Although I admit, it does sound familiar.

Two weeks ago, I wrote a reflection entitled "Patterns" about my grief and my thoughts on continuing to wear my wedding ring. The post seemed to strike a chord with everyone. It quickly became the most read reflection on my blog, beating out the previous leader, "Macc."

Readers commented, texted, and emailed me their experiences with their loved ones. Whether it was the loss of a parent or a spouse, they shared the many different approaches and feelings associated with this deeply personal decision.

The response took me by surprise, as I had very mixed feelings about whether to even publish something so personal about a topic with so many differing viewpoints. I did not want anyone to think I was judging them or their decisions.

My Joy Journey with Amy has made my life an open book. It has laid bare my vast love for Amy and exposed the deep pain of our family's loss.

I've talked quite a bit about the benefits of my hiking but have not directly addressed the therapeutic benefits of writing *My Joy Journey with Amy*. Whenever I find myself alone with my thoughts, I pull out my laptop and start writing the next reflection. This is especially helpful when the weather keeps me off the trails. It gives me focus and distracts me from my feelings of loss.

Last night, someone asked me how many reflections I have in queue at any given time. I generally have three or four lined up and ready to be published at any given moment. Most of the time that means that by the time they read a reflection, it is how I was feeling or thinking six weeks ago.

It also gives me a four-to-six-week grace period to generate the next story if I get busy or have writer's block. So far, I haven't had an issue generating additional stories as new ideas pop into my head from a memory with Amy or I have something I want to share about my grief journey.

Lately I have been feeling a lot like Carson did those many years ago. That I am not moving forward. I feel like I need a kick in the derriere to at least envision what I want my life after Amy to look like.

I am still bound to my grief daily and am just trying to get through each day and each week as best I can. Planning for the future is still tied to that fundamental goal.

A couple of weeks ago, a friend from pickleball asked me if I was dating yet. They apparently had a single friend. It caught me off guard. That was the first time I have been asked that question.

I really did not know how to respond, so I decided honesty was the best answer.

"I am always open to new friendships," I said. "But I am not ready for a romantic relationship."

The episode got me thinking of the larger picture. At some point I need to start thinking about how I want to live the rest of my life. The one I envisioned with Amy is no longer possible.

What do I want this new life to look like? What do I want to accomplish? Even, where do I want to live it? I wish I had an atlas for my life to show me the path forward. It has been eighteen months since Amy passed away. Like my advice to Carson, I am beginning to feel the need to shift my mindset. But I also consider it progress that I have at least finally asked myself these questions. Even if I have no idea how to answer them.

May 6, 2024 | Miles Hiked: 1,866

A LARGE MOTH

AMY AND I DID our best to expose our kids to the wonder and beauty of our country. From the Great Smoky Mountains to the Rocky Mountains, from the Black Hills and Badlands to the coast of Maine, we loved spending time outdoors hiking and camping.

Our trips, however, were always blessed with funny and irreverent moments that other families did not seem to share. For example, on one occasion, Amy was taking a shift driving through Iowa on our way to Rocky Mountain National Park. The Ford Expedition was packed to the gills with provisions so much so that we added a car top carrier for the extra toys and games we might need on our trip.

As we were tooling down the freeway at 70 miles per hour, one of the kids suddenly noticed there was a basketball and volleyball bouncing behind the car in the middle of the freeway. Given we were the only non-semi in the vicinity, we assumed something must have happened to our car top carrier.

Amy quickly pulled over to the side of the road to verify these items were from our car. Upon inspection, we realized the lock on the car top carrier had failed, and we were lucky to have only lost a couple of items. A quick detour to the nearest town for bungee cords fixed the problem.

Our trip to Glacier National Park a few years earlier, however, was one of our more memorable trips. The first day of travel was a harbinger of things to come as we had to navigate severe weather through the Twin Cities on our way to the first night's campground near Fargo. Our goal the second day was to reach Nashua, Montana, before completing our drive to Glacier National Park.

Our reservation the second night was for El Rancho Campground just outside of the town of Nashua. As we pulled into the "campground," we realized it was little more than someone's front lawn with a Porta-John in the yard. After a quick consultation with our travel partners, we mutually agreed there was no way we were staying there. We renamed the place "El Roncho" and decided to drive an extra forty-five minutes to an Army Corps of Engineers campground on Fort Peck Lake.

The unanticipated extra drive time made the passengers unruly and impatient after a long day's drive, but we arrived at the campground and were lucky enough to procure two sites. While I set up our popup camper, Amy took the kids exploring to the dam and the playground just a few campsites away.

We had the opportunity to relax around a small fire after dinner. As dusk descended, we noticed that a few bats began to dive bomb our campsite. They were obviously feeding on the local mosquito population, but it made us nervous. They literally flew within inches of us as we sat around the campfire.

What made us particularly uneasy was that a woman in Wisconsin had just been bitten by a bat that summer and developed rabies. Her case was covered extensively by the media because doctors used an untested method to fight the virus. They suppressed her brain function to give her immune system time to attack the virus. She is the only known survivor of the rabies virus that had progressed to its later stages.

As the light faded, we decided to return to our campers for the night to avoid the bats and get a good night's rest before the last leg of our drive to Glacier National Park.

As per usual about 2:00 a.m., nature called. I sleepily left the camper for the outdoor facilities. I returned to the camper and snuggled back into my sleeping bag next to Amy. She and the kids were fast asleep.

As I attempted to drift back off, I felt a disturbance in the force. I opened my eyes to take in the darkness and thought I detected a blur whip by my face. When it happened for a second time, I woke Amy.

"What?" she asked.

"Do you see a large moth flying by our heads?"

She paused and waited. The next time it passed, she screamed, "That's a bat!"

I jumped out of bed to turn the light on. With the recent story of the young woman from Fond du Lac fresh in our minds, we yelled at the kids to crawl to the bottom of their sleeping bags and stay there.

I grabbed the broom that was sitting by the door and with one foot holding the door open tried to direct the bat out of the camper. If I only had video of the chaos of me trying to swat the bat out the door, I am sure it would have garnered thousands of views on YouTube. After only a few minutes, the bat escaped our camper, and we all breathed a sigh of relief.

The rest of the trip was uneventful, and beautiful. Highlights included a hike up to a mountain lake, whitewater rafting, and a drive up Going-to-the-Sun Road.

On the rafting trip, the guide offered everyone an opportunity to take a swim. Claire, our swimmer, wanted to go in, so Amy felt obligated to join her. When Amy jumped into the river, the ice-cold water took her breath away. She surfaced and let out a scream. I am not sure what she expected, but the water was probably ice just a few hours earlier.

As I recall these trips, I find myself extremely grateful for the funky and unusual happenings. It is interesting that I remember and cherish these moments more than the breathtaking views and scenery. I wouldn't trade them for anything. Embrace the weirdness; they are memories etched in gold.

May 20, 2024 | Miles Hiked: 1,917

DUPA

AS A NATURAL BORN skeptic, I was always dubious when I heard tales of women craving pickles or ice cream or some other food during their pregnancies. I just did not put much stock into such stories—until Amy was pregnant with Claire, that is.

One night, I cut up an entire watermelon for us to enjoy either as a snack or with dinner. I put it in the refrigerator and proceeded to move on to another chore. When I returned to the kitchen about an hour later, I found Amy enjoying the watermelon. I did not think much of it until later that night when I noticed the empty container in the dishwasher. Amy had eaten an entire watermelon in less than two hours. Not one of those mini watermelons either, but a full-sized one.

When I teased her, she denied eating the entire watermelon, but given it was just her and me at the time, it was not difficult to deduce the truth. She also asked me to go to the store and pick up another one. As cravings go, this was a pretty healthy one, and it continued for the entire pregnancy.

Several years later when she was pregnant with the twins, her iron levels were low. The doctor recommended Amy eat liver. That was a hard no for Amy, but she substituted liverwurst sandwiches instead. In this case, she craved these sandwiches topped with pickle slices and had them at least twice each day.

In my grief, I find I crave many things about my relationship with Amy. I miss them terribly.

I crave to see her smile and to hear her laugh. I crave to have her next to me on the couch falling asleep while watching a television show. I crave to see her dance anytime the mood struck her. I crave to hear her wisdom when the kids come to me for advice.

I crave to see her cry while watching a sad movie. It always reminded me to be more empathetic to people's pain and circumstances and to appreciate our many blessings.

I crave to hear her call me a *dupa*, Polish slang for little ass, which was mostly used affectionately when I did something stupid or careless. Like my many mishaps with ladders.

I crave so many, many things about Amy.

One of the more enduring is that I crave to rub her arm at night. For some reason, Amy found great comfort in that gesture from me after she was diagnosed with cancer. I never really knew whether it was because it helped her relax, provided a counterbalance to her pain, or whether it made her feel less alone in her illness. She often needed it to help her fall asleep at night.

Her sister Mary once tried to relieve me of this duty for an evening only to be promptly fired from arm rubbing duty after only fifteen minutes.

Sometimes I would rub Amy's arm for hours as she slept. If I stopped from exhaustion, she would often wake up and ask me to rub her arm again not realizing I had been doing it the past two hours in the darkness.

Now after more than a year and a half, I still reflexively reach out for her arm each night only to find the cold sheet.

I guess I just crave her presence. The way we communicated with a single word, gesture, or look. The way we always seemed to be in sync. It is so lonely without her.

If she were here, I imagine she would smile, brush my cheek with her hand, call me a dupa, and gently nudge me forward toward my new life. But I have found that first step to be the hardest.

June 3, 2024 | Miles Hiked: 1,953

A NEW STAR

ANYONE WHO IS LUCKY enough to be present when their children are born knows the wonder and magnificence of that moment. I was blessed to be present for the birth of all three of our children, and they were unforgettable. Words can never convey the emotions and love present as your child enters the world.

With our first child, we had no idea what to expect. The trend back in 1994 was to give birth without the assistance of pain medication. During our Lamaze classes, the instructor practically shamed couples who indicated they weren't going to have a *natural* childbirth experience. Given it was our first child, we—meaning Amy—decided to forgo the pain medications if possible.

At the forty-week appointment, the doctor saw no evidence that Amy was in labor, even though the baby had dropped a couple of weeks prior. We returned home disappointed.

The next day, Amy called me at work to let me know she was *feeling* something. I headed home just in case. When I arrived, there was still no movement and those *feelings* had dissipated.

Amy had heard that walking sometimes could hasten childbirth, so the rest of the afternoon and evening we could be seen walking slowly through our neighborhood. By 9:00 p.m., we were both exhausted and decided to try and get some sleep in case those feelings returned in the middle of the night.

At some point in the night, Amy woke me as she was feeling contractions. We timed them, but they were roughly seven to eight minutes apart. Being first-time parents, we decided that was good enough, and we called the doctor on duty about 4:00 a.m. They told us very gently that was great, but not to head to the hospital until the contractions were about four to five minutes apart or they lasted more than a minute.

By 6:30 a.m., we were both anxious to get the show rolling, so we headed to the hospital. Once we arrived and settled into our room, the contractions continued to be spaced out. Amy was increasingly uncomfortable as the morning dragged on and the contractions increased in intensity. The nurse suggested Amy try to relax by resting in a hot tub.

While she was in the hot tub, she closed her eyes and was very peaceful. I made a note to thank the nurse for her suggestion as it seemed to be working very well. After ten minutes, Amy suddenly opened her eyes, looked confused, and then asked me how long she had been passed out.

She never really forgave me for my assumption that she was meditating and gave me grief about it every time we recalled the incident.

At that point, she decided that she wanted an epidural for the pain. Unfortunately, her medical team said that it was too late in the process, and she would need to proceed without anything to manage the pain. She squeezed my hand so hard during the contractions that she bent my wedding ring.

The contractions continued to grow in intensity and began to accelerate quickly. It was then that the baby's vitals began to show signs of distress. The medical team started moving with haste to prepare for an emergency C-section.

Her medical team moved Amy to various positions in hopes of relieving the stress on our little one. They were able to find a very awkward position that seemed to help. Amy was focused and told the staff she could maintain the very uncomfortable pose as long as needed. She was able to maintain her position for about fifteen minutes before the contractions reached a point where her team said it was time for Amy to deliver the baby.

The rest of the delivery was a blur; however, I remembered the most important task of any husband present at their child's birth: Do as you're told and don't get in the way.

Claire Louise arrived at 1:56 p.m. on a beautiful October afternoon. She weighed six pounds, seven ounces. A new star was born.

A few days later, I lay on the couch with Claire Bear asleep on my chest. I watched as her breath went in and out and realized in that moment that I had never been closer to heaven.

June 17, 2024 | Miles Hiked: 1,953

SURROUNDED

AFTER AMY'S CANCER DIAGNOSIS, I was determined to share some of my favorite places with her. I am not sure why I felt compelled to ensure Amy visited these beautiful and exotic locations, but it was important to me. One of those destinations was Yellowstone National Park and the Grand Tetons.

Amy and I discussed and agreed that we did not want to put our life on hold indefinitely. So just a few months after she began chemo, we decided to plan a trip to these famous destinations, assuming progress could be made with her cancer markers.

Keeping with the Year of No Budget theme, we spared no

expense. We decided to fly to Cody, Wyoming, where Mary and Jerry would pick us up at the airport and take us into the park. This allowed for the transport of *the contraption* to our destination and allowed us to take the additional supplies we would need.

Camping was out of the question, so we jumped on getting reservations at various lodges within the park early to make sure Amy would be comfortable and have a place to rest after a day of sightseeing.

We caught a connecting flight in Denver, and as we descended to Cody, Amy clutched my arm tight. She had never flown into such a small airport surrounded by mountains and was afraid we were going to crash until the runway suddenly appeared below the plane, and we touched down.

Our ride was waiting as planned, and we wasted no time getting on the road into Yellowstone. Over the next ten days, we visited many of the park's attractions, including Lamar Valley, Mammoth Hot Springs, the Geyser Basin, the Grand Canyon of the Yellowstone, Old Faithful, and many more.

Late in our journey, Yellowstone was overwhelmed by flooding from the record snow melt and rain. We were eventually evacuated from the park late one evening just as we were winding down for the night. Fortunately, our lodge in Jackson at the base of the Teton mountain range was able to take us in a day early as we shifted south.

The Tetons were breathtaking, and we enjoyed a slow ride through the park, learned to fly fish on a local river, fished on Jackson Lake, and stopped at many local shops.

Unfortunately, with her compromised immune system, Amy fell ill to COVID the last day or two of our trip and the journey home became a challenge. Several weeks later after she recovered, she spoke more fondly of the trip as we recalled some of the breathtaking views and memories together with Mary and Jerry.

About a month later, I was sharing some of the moments from our trip with my brother, Chuck. I expressed my disappointment that Amy did not seem to share my enthusiasm about seeing these places. He shared with me a different perspective.

"Over my career [in law enforcement], I have seen a lot of sad situations, including many individuals who were at the end of their journeys," he said. "I have found that most people don't care about what they haven't seen or done. What they care about the most in those moments is being surrounded by the people they love."

Three months later, I would remember those words. As Amy's disease progressed rapidly, she was surrounded by our family. Although she was not conscious the last forty-eight hours, with one exception, I know she felt every hand that held hers and every kiss planted on her forehead. We read to her the outpouring of love and support communicated to us by friends, colleagues, neighbors, and acquaintances. I am sure she appreciated hearing every word.

As I forge ahead with this new life, I vow to remember my brother's wise words. I will not sacrifice time with family and friends in a quest to hike the longest trail or see the most beautiful sunset. Instead, I hope to be side-by-side with them. To be surrounded. To love and be loved.

July 1, 2024 | Miles Hiked: 1,958

BINARY

A **PREVIOUS REFLECTION DETAILED THE** unusual circumstances of Amy's pregnancy with Morgan and Carson, our Mo-Mo twins. That story omits one other complication experienced during her pregnancy. Just after we received the fantastic news that the boys were not Mo-Mo twins, Amy had a seizure and was diagnosed with epilepsy.

In the state of Wisconsin, an unexplained loss of consciousness requires the temporary suspension of your driver's license for a period of three months with no exceptions.

In the era prior to working remote, this was incredibly inconvenient because Amy worked forty-five minutes from our home. Fortunately, Sue, a colleague who lived close by, stepped up and offered to drive Amy to work every morning. The only condition placed on this generous offer was that Amy had to promise not to go into labor during her commute.

Amy was not due until mid-January, but the doctor warned us that twins often come earlier than forty weeks. Then one morning in December, Amy woke up with a very bad backache. She took some ibuprofen before Sue picked her up, but she insisted on going to work.

Her backache worsened on the way. Sue instructed Amy to move her seat position all the way back and to try and relax. It did not work. After they arrived at the office, Amy proceeded to throw up in every sink on the way to her desk. Sue gently suggested to Amy that she was in labor, but Amy was doubtful because it did not feel like her labor with Claire.

I raced to pick her up, as regardless of cause, she should not have been at work. While we were on our way home, I asked her to try and focus on the source of her pain. "Where does it originate?" I asked.

It was then that Amy finally realized that the pains were contractions. We timed them while we were driving and found them to be only forty-five seconds apart. We called the doctor and diverted to the hospital. Our anxiety was elevated as we pulled in. The staff took her up to the maternity ward while I was parking the car. By the time I arrived, they had made Amy comfortable, and she had calmed down. The contractions began to taper off and she was finally able to relax.

Six or seven hours later, the nurse informed us that Amy was still dilated only five centimeters. Amy felt the urge to push a couple of minutes later. We paged the nurse and shared this information. She told us that it was doubtful Amy was ready as she was only five centimeters just a few minutes ago. Upon inspection, however, the nurse exclaimed that Amy was fully dilated.

The nurse called into her phone and suddenly everything was a whirlwind of activity. They wanted Amy to deliver the twins in the operating room in case they needed to perform a C-section. Within two minutes, we were surrounded by four or five nurses, and they rolled Amy down the hallway to the operating room. At the entryway, they asked me to wait for another nurse so that I could get gowned up. As they wheeled Amy into the room, we made eye contact, and I could tell Amy was suddenly nervous.

I donned my gown and mask as quickly as possible so that I could rejoin Amy. When I entered the room, I could see Amy visibly relax when she saw me. I quickly moved to her side to hold her hand. This time, I took off my wedding ring so she could not bend the ring again.

The doctor entered the room and within minutes, Morgan arrived in the world at five pounds, eleven ounces. There was a complication with Carson, however. He was in the wrong position. The doctor asked that Amy not push. This was easier said than done. Amy and I looked at each other and we began to sing "Walking in a Winter Wonderland." The nurses looked at us like we were crazy. It must have been a first for their delivery room.

The doctor worked her magic and was able to turn Carson into position for delivery after about fifteen minutes, and he arrived soon after, also weighing in at five pounds, eleven ounces. The twins were within two-tenths of an ounce of each other. The doctor had never seen twins that close together in weight before.

As the years passed, Morgan and Carson were inseparable. Their worlds orbited around each other in all things. In the rare circumstances they had to go different directions for an evening, Amy and I found it hilarious that the first words either of them would utter upon entering the door were where's Morgan or where's Carson, never hello or hi, Mom and Dad.

Upon graduation, they were accepted to a variety of colleges. Carson was headed to a junior college in Iowa to play baseball. Amy, Claire, Morgan, and I had a very rare dinner out together without Carson. When we asked Morgan about his thoughts on where he wanted to go, he burst into tears and said he was not ready to leave his brother. Thus, they both spent their freshman year in college in the corn fields of Iowa before transferring to the University of Wisconsin-La Crosse the following year.

They pursued the same career in law enforcement, bought the same midnight blue Dodge Ram truck, and their first jobs out of college were both with the Madison Police Department. There is an uncanny connection between the two that I doubt will ever be broken. Their worlds truly are binary.

July 15, 2024 | Miles Hiked: 1,984

EMBRACE

A COUPLE OF WEEKS AGO, I had the opportunity to visit my college roommate Craig and his wife Jan during a visit to Minnesota. It is always great to get caught up with them and their busy lives. They are enjoying retirement and finding great joy in caring for their grandchildren.

They have also been taking time to travel the last couple of years and have visited many places that are on my bucket list. Their approach is almost the polar opposite of the approach Amy and I often took. They claim to have a destination in mind but make no definitive plans. No hotel reservations, no itinerary, no specific landmarks they want to visit. They get in the car and go, winging it.

To date, he says they have never been stranded or left to travel an extra fifty miles to find a hotel room. Spontaneity works perfectly for them, and they feel no stress about either making plans or meeting expectations.

I contemplated their approach to retirement. I thought to myself that the most important and meaningful moments of my life with Amy often were unplanned or impulsive. From going all-in and proposing to Amy after only knowing her five months to the blessing of having twin boys, one more than our plans called for, those impulsive and unexpected events enriched our lives. I could not imagine a life without these blessings and the joy these events brought to our life.

Later in that same visit, I had dinner with my brother, and he asked me, "How are you doing with Amy's loss?" A surprisingly frank and abrupt question from my typically reserved brother.

I shared with him my thoughts that I needed to make a change. That I felt stuck in my grief. That I wasn't making any progress in figuring out what I wanted to do with my new life. I was contemplating making a drastic change to get me moving forward. His response made an instant impression.

"You know, you don't have to figure it all out before you start," he said. "You can figure it out on the way."

My mind reeled. I had never considered that. I was looking for the perfect solution. I was waiting for an epiphany or revelation to help me envision a new future. A revelation that might never come. Chuck was saying that I could always change my mind or even start over.

Instead of waiting to figure it all out, I could just embrace the unknown.

I just need to pick a direction, any direction, and take that first step. I am such an idiot.

July 29, 2024 | Miles Hiked: 2,012

THE FLYING W RANCH

The following was taken from my eulogy for Amy. I added some details to round the story out and make it more complete. Seems fitting to include it here.

I MET AMY AT A work training for Junior Achievement in Colorado Springs. The training class was housed at the Cheyenne Mountain Inn at the base of Cheyenne Mountain, overlooking the Country Club of Colorado. It was a magnificent setting. We only had to walk across the parking lot to get to the national headquarters for Junior Achievement and their multifaceted training facility.

On the first day, we gathered in the training room full of fifty people arrayed in several long rows. There was one space where they squeezed in an extra table for two people. Fate brought our name plates to those two seats. We began to learn about each other. In our first get to know your colleague exercise, I learned that Amy had the most interesting job of anyone in the class. She had worked as Billy Bob from ShowBiz Pizza Place. She had donned the costume for multiple birthday parties and even walked in a parade as the beloved character.

I had met her colleague from Milwaukee, Steve, the day before the training started, and we began to eat our meals together along with another colleague from Toledo, Ohio. I had met him years earlier when I had attended the National Junior Achievement Conference (NAJAC) as a sophomore in high school. It was astounding to me that he could remember me from one week ten or twelve years earlier.

Amy and I spent most of our free time outside of training with each other, including a whitewater rafting trip to the Royal Gorge on a day off and nights by the hotel pool. One night, Junior Achievement arranged for an outing to the Flying W Ranch where we enjoyed a chuck wagon dinner and show. As we strolled around the property after dinner, I began to realize that I was attracted to Amy's smile, positive attitude, and genuine interest in my life.

Before dinner the next night, I asked her to take a walk with me through the golf course. We wandered down the paths, and she shared many of her family traditions with me.

On the night before our last day of training and our subsequent flights home, Junior Achievement sponsored an outing to a local restaurant and dance club. I was a bit shy, wondering if I had been too inquisitive the day before. I decided to give her more space and hung out with one of our other colleagues and enjoyed a conversation while most of our fellow associates hit the dance floor. Dancing is not my forte, but it is one of Amy's. She soon found me hiding in the corner and dragged me out to the dance floor. She was not put off when I confessed I wasn't a good dancer.

The next day we exchanged numbers and vowed to stay in touch. In St. Louis, I briefly connected with my regional manager, JT Williams. He was also my mentor in the organization and a good friend. I shared my experience at the training session and mentioned meeting Amy. I said I wanted to call her in a couple of weeks.

He said, "No. Don't wait. Call her this week."

It was the best advice anyone has ever given me.

I called Amy a couple of days later and asked if I could visit her in Milwaukee. I was a little taken aback when she told me she would get back to me. Several days later, I received a voice message from her saying she would like me to visit. She apologized for her response and said she was still living at home and wanted to discuss any visit with her parents in advance.

Encouraged, I booked a flight for a weekend in September and gave her my flight information. I decided I best not show up empty-handed, so I bought a stuffed white polar bear about the same size as Macc. The stuffed bear occupied the seat next to me on the plane and many strangers commented on him as they boarded.

After landing, I eagerly headed to the baggage claim area where we had agreed to meet with my bear in hand. Amy was not there.

I waited . . . and waited . . . and waited.

As I began to formulate a plan to make the most of my visit to Milwaukee, Amy finally arrived. Her volunteer training had run long. She walked right up to me, and without saying a single word, she gave me a kiss.

Only three months later, we were engaged and embarked on our thirty-two-year joy journey together.

I lost touch with JT over the years, but I will be eternally grateful for his firm encouragement to call Amy.

Fast forward thirty-two years. Complications from Amy's cancer had progressed and our entire family knew the moment we were dreading was coming. As she took her last breath, I witnessed a moment of bittersweet joy as Carson, Morgan, and Claire demonstrated their pure love for Amy. It is a moment I will both hate and cherish for the rest of my life. I know with absolute certainty that Amy and I have brought three wonderful, beautiful individuals into this world. The world will most definitely be a better place as a result of her unconditional love and support for them.

My healing journey will be long and difficult, but how can I not elect to live up to Amy's example to choose joy each and every day. Amy would want all of those she loves and cares for to do the same.

August 12, 2024 | Miles Hiked: 2,061

JOY AND HOPE

A **S I SIT DOWN** to write this final reflection for *My Joy Journey with Amy*, I have very mixed emotions. I know with certainty that my grief journey has not ended. As I have reiterated multiple times throughout my writings, loss is a profound life-changing event that has no end. There will be no congratulations from family and friends that I have somehow made it through the worst of my grief. In many ways, I suspect that I am still at the beginning of this journey.

But I also know with certainty that Amy would never want me to be so immersed in grief that I ignore the daily opportunities to choose joy in my life and to spread joy to others. You may have sensed an inflection point in my writings where I have begun looking forward more than recounting my wonderful memories of my life with Amy. I have so many more stories of our lives together, but I know she would be starting to get annoyed with me at all the mushy expressions of my love for her contained in my writings. She was a very private person, and although she certainly would have cut me some slack, I have heard her whispering in my ear to transition to something less focused on her.

Many of the details of how we met and began our courtship are contained in other portions of this book. But our love story truly began in Colorado. On the first weekend we met, we were afforded a day off from our training at Junior Achievement. A group of us chose to use the day to whitewater raft down the Arkansas River and the Royal Gorge. We were both financially strapped at the time, but neither of us could pass up the opportunity for this once in a lifetime experience.

After Amy passed, I envisioned a trip back to the Arkansas River with Claire, Morgan, and Carson to share with them this most wonderful memory of where our love first took root. I invited other members of our family and was surprised when everyone accepted my invitation. Altogether, fourteen members of our family made the journey to Canon City, Colorado, for a three-day, two-night camping excursion down seventy miles of the Arkansas River.

Yes, we had some bittersweet moments where we were missing our loved ones. Tears flowed and hugs were shared. But I also believe it was the experience of a lifetime. What better way to honor Amy and our other lost loved ones than to choose joy by experiencing the scenic wonder of the Royal Gorge.

As the time for this adventure neared, I felt more and more convinced that it was the right time to conclude *My Joy Journey with Amy*. I contemplated this final chapter and continued to wrestle with the question what's next? Writing and hiking have been my therapy. I could not see myself giving up on either. So, I began to formulate a plan to transition to a new initiative, *My Joy Journey of Hope*.

Like Amy's focus on *joy*, I have always been captivated by the concept and stories of *hope*. That includes my all-time favorite movie *Shawshank Redemption*. I share Andy Dufresne's view of hope: "Hope is a good thing, maybe the best of things, and no good thing ever dies."

Hope is essential in our darkest hours. It helps us find resilience to overcome loss, adversity, or pessimism and to strive for something better. Thus, *My Joy Journey of Hope* felt like the perfect fit.

At this point I do not know what I will be writing about. Probably more of the same, but with more emphasis on looking forward than looking back. Amy is, and will always be, the love of my life, but I have felt her urging me forward the past few months.

Like everyone, I have no idea what the future holds. But instead of being immersed in my grief each day, I want to wake up with the morning sun shining on my face with a daily mission to find joy and hope.

It has given me great comfort to share my thoughts and emotions with all of you over the past two years. Words cannot express my gratitude for your willingness to make this journey with me. I am hopeful many of you will also choose to follow my new blog *My Joy Journey of Hope* (www.myjoyjourneyofhope.com).

Cheers.

ACKNOWLEDGMENTS

I would like to thank my family, Claire, Morgan, Carson, and Hayley, for giving me the material to create this tribute to Amy and for their support for my writing. I started this endeavor as a therapeutic exercise to help me with my grief. It has morphed into something so much more and has become an integral part of my life. It provided an outlet to express my love for Amy, the most wonderful wife, mother, and friend. Thank you to the four of them for reading my reflections, providing input, and always encouraging me to continue.

My book designer, Becky Bayne, and editor, Melissa Stevens, also deserve accolades for putting up with my distractions and for working to make *My Joy Journey with Amy* the best it could be. In the early stages of developing this book, I thought the book was a record of my life together with Amy along with a journal of my grief journey. Becky pointed out to me that it was more than that. It was a love story. Thank you for framing this initiative in that light.

I would also like to thank several others for their support along the way, Joe, Jackie, Jim, Michelle, Chuck, Doris, Mary, Jerry, Jody, all of my pickleball and curling friends, and the countless others who have given me their support for writing and hiking on this journey.

Thank you, also, to the strangers I met out on the trail or in the most random places who listened to my stories with kindness and understanding.

Special acknowledgement to Katlyn Roloff of Katibee Photography for the beautiful cover photo. No picture captures Amy's spirit of joy more than this photo. Katlyn also took the chapter heading photo of Claire and Amy in "Miss Independent, Part 2."

Most of all, I wish to thank Amy. You provided my life with so much joy and happiness. I will be forever thankful to you for being the love of my life. I hope you are proud of me for trying to choose and spread joy every day. I love you now and forever.

AUTHOR BIO

MARK YOUNGQUIST IS AN explorer, writer, and wanderer. After the passing of the love of his life, Amy, he took up hiking and writing as a mechanism to cope with his loss. Most days you can find him hiking a trail, playing pickleball, or curling. Mark loves his family and friends fiercely and seeks to choose joy and hope every day.

Follow Mark's blog at www.myjoyjourneywithamy.com

25% of this book's proceeds go to the American Cancer Society and another 25% to go to the Ice Age Trail Alliance.

ANNOUNCING

MY JOY JOURNEY OF HOPE

Follow Mark's new blog at

www.myjoyjourneyofhope.com

www.ingramcontent.com/pod-product-compliance
Lightning Source LLC
Chambersburg PA
CBHW051617120626
46551CB00014B/1834